PLAYING GOD'S MELODIES

JANE MILWARD

Playing God's melodies

The psalms in our lives

ST PAULS

Acknowledgements. My thanks are due especially to the past and present chaplains of Westminster Cathedral and editors of the *Westminster Cathedral Bulletin* who encouraged me to write about the psalms. I also acknowledge help received from *The Jerome Biblical Commentary* edited by Raymond E. Brown SS, Joseph A. Fitzmyer SJ, and Roland E. Murphy O.Carm. (Geoffrey Chapman, 1986); and Martin Israel, *A Light on the Path* (Darton, Longman and Todd, 1990). The last paragraph of Chapter 10 is from *Words of Encouragement* edited by Daniel Cronin (St Pauls, 1992).

Psalms and the *Magnificat* are taken from *The Psalms: A New Translation* published by Harper Collins and from *The Divine Office* by permission of A.P. Watt Ltd on behalf of The Grail, England.

Scripture quotations are taken from *The Jerusalem Bible*, published and copyright 1966, 1967 and 1968 by Darton, Longman and Todd Ltd and Doubleday & Co Inc, and used by permission.

Cover illustration: *David playing the harp*. Add MS11639 folio 117 verso. By permission of the British Library

ST PAULS
Middlegreen, Slough SL3 6BT, United Kingdom
Moyglare Road, Maynooth, Co, Kildare, Ireland

© ST PAULS 1994

ISBN 085439 465 6

Printed by The Guernsey Press Ltd, Guernsey, C.I.

St PAULS is an activity of the priests and brothers of the Society of St Paul who proclaim the Gospel through the media of social communication

Contents

Foreword

It is surely true to say that the fulness of life is reflected in the Psalms. They have an amazing ability to meet the deepest needs of people from one generation to the next; they seem to resonate so realistically with our own lived experience.

One result of the Second Vatican Council was to further the study and appreciation of the Scriptures as a whole. Except for priests and Religious, though, the book of poems called the Psalms still remained less understood and valued by people in this country. However, in 1963 The Grail had translated their texts from the Hebrew. In 1966 a 'singing version' was brought out, and it was incorporated into the 1974 revised and simplified form of the Divine Office. That official prayer of the Church had evolved over the centuries. Orders of monks and nuns such as the Benedictines had been founded to make the chanting or recitation of the Office one of their chief daily works. Today lay people are increasingly being attracted to it as well.

In this book, Jane Milward, a parishioner of Westminster Cathedral, writes with the experience of someone who has been greatly helped by praying and meditating on the psalms. It seems to me this book has a particular value in that she courageously shares with the reader a great deal from her personal life.

Some sections have already appeared in the *Westminster Cathedral Bulletin*, where they aroused some interest. I hope that this book may, in its turn, also prove fruitful, and I warmly recommend it to you.

Daniel P. Cronin
Chancellor
Diocese of Westminster

Introduction

How easy is it for us to open out to God when in practice we find it difficult to accept his unconditional love for us? Can we tell him all about our lives including our various problems, trivial as well as big, and our confused feelings or emotional states? Doing that with another human being can result in a sense of release. Equally, it can be exhilarating to find when reading that others have had ideas, troubles or experiences in life similar to ours.

This can apply in our relationship with God. Others may be able to show us how to try to give our lives more fully to him. It is widely accepted that the psalmists can be of particular help. Their words were divinely inspired, and through them the Holy Spirit can speak to us today. The following quotations might perhaps have helped you when praying to God at different times in your life:

> Give heed to my groaning (Ps 5).
> A humbled, contrite heart you will not spurn (Ps 50).
> I will praise you, Lord, you have rescued me (Ps 29).

Those examples were taken from one week (the first) of the four-week cycle of psalms in the Morning and Evening Prayer of the Church. A rather different example, however, occurs in the second week:

> Since you, O God, are my stronghold,
> why have you rejected me? (Ps 42)

Without piling up quotations, there can be found expressed in the 150 psalms an extremely broad range of honest, human emotions with regard to God, ranging from praise and wonder, thanksgiving, joy and trust, to petition, sorrow, questioning, fear and even desolation. The psalms

9

were composed in Old Testament times, and were used then and by Jesus and Mary, his mother, as well as by countless believers since. They form the backbone of the present-day revised Divine Office, in which the Morning and Evening Prayer (the former Lauds and Vespers) are the chief 'hours' (or parts).

Since they originated in the pre-Christian era, the psalms cannot be expected to convey to us the full Christian message. Some points should be noted in particular. The psalmists did not know that there are three Persons in God. The Jews thought that God's blessing and favour were shown by material prosperity, length of life and numerous offspring. They were uncertain about whether there is life after death.

Despite the unavoidable omissions, there is much to encourage us. Some themes especially relevant to the Jewish people keep recurring, such as how to react when in distress of any kind and how to turn to God. The individuality and the humanity of the psalmists often appear. There is a timelessness about these writings, and it is wonderful to reflect that they helped to develop the spiritual life of Christ himself.

Sudden changes of mood or of subject-matter can take place. While these may sometimes leave the reader perplexed, they can, almost surprisingly, help prayer. When our minds wander, a different approach can bring us back to attend to the book before us. Further, one psalm may be applied to many different occasions or feast days, but that can make it harder to classify.

This book originated in a series of articles for the *Westminster Cathedral Bulletin*. They were written partly to encourage Catholics to join in the Morning and Evening Prayer of the Church. In selecting further psalms for the present work, preference continued to be given to psalms included in those Prayers. The shorter psalms are usually printed here in full, but only extracts are given for most of the longer ones.

After prayer, each psalm gave to me an idea of how I

might approach it, sometimes very personally. Occasionally it seemed best to concentrate on one aspect which had struck me. I did not follow any preconceived plan. So, arranging the final pieces to make a whole was rather a challenge. However, my hope is that, with the help of the indexes, you will find it easy to dip into this book should you not wish to read it straight through, and also that you will be led to ponder on and to pray the psalms for yourselves.

A final technical matter is that there are two numbering systems for the psalms: the Greek Septuagint and the Hebrew. For most numbers, the Greek (used in this book) is one less than the Hebrew system. This explains why 'The Lord is my shepherd' is known to some people as Psalm 22 but to others as Psalm 23.

1

The Magnificat

On a February morning, I was walking past a fruit stall at the corner of a street, not thinking about anything in particular. Suddenly, some words dropped, as it were, into my mind:

Our life, like a bird, has escaped
from the snare of the fowler.

They were from Psalm 123, and perfectly summed up my situation at the time.

For a couple of years I had been faced with a serious moral problem and considerable pressure had been brought to bear on me. The strain had been great, but the solution was unexpected and wonderful and had only recently come. It was surely the Holy Spirit who had brought those words from my subconscious and put them into the forefront of my mind.

Mary is the sinless Mother of God. She, even more than her cousin Elizabeth, was filled with the Holy Spirit when, quite soon after the annunciation, she proclaimed her song of praise of God, the *Magnificat* (Lk 1:46-55):

My soul glorifies the Lord,
my spirit rejoices in God, my Saviour.
He looks on his servant in her lowliness;
henceforth all ages will call me blessed.

The Almighty works marvels for me.
Holy his name!
His mercy is from age to age,
on those who fear him.

He puts forth his arm in strength
and scatters the proud-hearted.
He casts the mighty from their thrones
and raises the lowly.

He fills the starving with good things,
sends the rich away empty.

He protects Israel, his servant,
remembering his mercy,
the mercy promised to our fathers,
to Abraham and his sons for ever.

The *Magnificat* contains allusions to at least four psalms.
In it, Mary at her visitation pours out her adoration, joy,
gratitude and wonder at God's condescension in having
become incarnate in her womb. She is looking at God, not
at herself. She is amazed that he had first looked on her for,
as a genuinely humble person, she knows that she is only a
creature of his. In quick succession, she touches on several
themes which are frequently found in the psalms: praise of
God for himself and for his wonderful works; his mercy,
shown to those who fear him; his reversal of ordinary
human values, so that the poor, the needy and the humble
are raised; his continued protection of his people; and his
absolute faithfulness.

Mary would have meditated on the psalms from her
childhood. As a result, she instinctively called on her knowledge of them at a crucial time in her life. They could reflect
very deep thoughts, feelings and emotions within her. Later,
she would have taught them to her Son, Jesus. The gospels
show that he, in turn, used phrases from the psalms, not
least during his crucifixion.

We, of course, lack Mary's special gifts: her freedom
from original sin, her full co-operation with the Holy Spirit,
and her divine motherhood. However, we can make some
parts of the *Magnificat* our own, for God in Christ has
saved us too. Those words of hers which particularly seem
to me to speak directly to us today are:

14

His mercy is from age to age,
on those who fear him.

'Mercy' is a translation of the Latin word *misericordia*, which can also be translated as pity which inclines a person to help another, as compassion, or as merciful love. Those words will always describe God's unchanging attitude towards us, but we need to have a proper reverence for him, as Mary had. That kind of 'fear' is a gift of the Holy Spirit, and 'to fear the Lord is the first stage of wisdom' (Ps 110; see Ch. 45).

Our attitude to God has to be one of dependence, for we are his creatures, but also, as Christ taught us, one of relationship. That relationship is in the family of love, between Father and children where, ultimately, God's love, being so great and inexhaustible, will cast out any inappropriate fear on our side. As John wrote: 'In love there can be no fear, but fear is driven out by perfect love' (1 Jn 4:18).

We are sinners, and we all need God's mercy and forgiveness. Gradually, though, the more we open out to him, with Mary's help, the more we shall experience the truth of his love.

2

Interpretation of psalms

There is a priest who is usually relaxed and has a pleasant
sense of humour. Once I heard him reading at Mass from
Mark's gospel. By the end of the passage, I found that I
was inwardly laughing, and that surprised me. I had heard
that reading before, and surely we should be solemn at the
gospel! Later, I had a chance to speak to him. Yes, he did
find that particular extract amusing, and also other parts of
the same gospel. He could bring a new slant to his reading
of Mark's gospel, and that interpretation was conveyed to
his listeners.

It is possible to have somewhat similar experiences with
the interpretation of the psalms. The Church can help us to
find different meanings and a new significance in them.
For example, Psalm 147 is often used in the Office:

O praise the Lord, Jerusalem!
Sion, praise your God!

He has strengthened the bars of your gates,
he has blessed the children within you.
He established peace on your borders,
he feeds you with finest wheat.

He sends out his word to the earth
and swiftly runs his command.
He showers down snow white as wool,
he scatters hoar-frost like ashes.

He hurls down hailstones like crumbs.
The waters are frozen at his touch;

he sends forth his word and it melts them:
at the breath of his mouth the waters flow.

He makes his word known to Jacob,
to Israel his laws and decrees.
He has not dealt thus with other nations;
he has not taught them his decrees.

God's people are repeatedly invited to join in praise for all that he has done.

For the Jews, this psalm was one of a group to be recited in the mornings. It must have helped to encourage them, for it reminded them that the all-powerful God, the creator and master of nature and of the universe, had singled them out to care for them as his own chosen people.

For Christians, a striking feature of the psalm is its frequent use of 'word': God sends out his word to the earth; he sends his word to melt the frozen waters; he makes his word (this time, meaning ordinances) known to Jacob.

John in his gospel expanded on his idea that Christ is the Word of God, who was sent by the Father into the world. For Christ to have become man, God had depended on the 'Fiat', the word of assent, of Mary, who had been especially chosen and prepared to become the mother of his Son. Before Christmas, we can tend to feel rather like frozen waters, needing melting. Every Christmas, we are touched again by the knowledge that God in Christ was born as a fragile human baby, with all the limitations that that involved. He could not even react much to his surroundings, but was again dependent on his mother.

The life's work of Jesus was to call people to repentance and to belief in the Good News of salvation. Men rejected him and crucified him. The details of his public ministry, selflessly spent in teaching and in caring for others, followed by his unjust trial, sufferings and death, have been and are enough to influence and change the lives of countless millions.

Christ is the Second Person of the Blessed Trinity, and

17

the psalm can be interpreted as relating to all three: God the Father sent his Son and melted waters at the breath of his mouth, that is, by the Holy Spirit. Further, the mention of our being fed with finest wheat suggests to us the Holy Eucharist, which is not, though, wheat, or the finest wheat. It is Christ himself, the food for our souls.

It is hardly surprising that Psalm 147 is recited in the Office on the following days: the Annunciation, Christmas Day, Good Friday, the Triumph of the Cross, Trinity Sunday, Corpus Christi (the Body and Blood of Christ) and All Saints Day, as well as on alternate Fridays. When it is prayerfully said on one of these occasions and in the context of the feast, with a special 'antiphon' (an introductory sentence from Scripture), it can take on a different quality and meaning, and so help to touch our own hearts.

3

God's omniscience

When you were a small child, did you ever meet an adult (maybe an unusual visitor at your home) who silently looked you over critically, and then ignored you but made to your parents an adverse comment about you which you could easily hear and understand? A child would naturally find that comment unfair and hurtful.

Adults who get on well with children value them as persons, and enjoy watching them and spending time with them. In return, the children would sense love and the trust placed in them, and they would respond, for some time at least. They could relax and play, without attending to those watching eyes.

God, our Father, is like such an adult or, rather, such adults resemble him. He does not keep trying to detect whether we are misbehaving in some important matter, let alone in some insignificant way. He does not study us through some ancient quizzing-glass. Although it can be hard for us to satisfy his plans for us, he loves us always and is always interested in us whatever happens. Humanly speaking, that interest surely extends to his finding kindly amusement at some of our antics; he cannot take his eyes off us.

The first part of Psalm 138 expresses that beautifully and fervently. It is written personally, in a manner suggestive of experience. The psalmist directly addresses God throughout in a familiar but highly respectful way. Other psalms are written impersonally and speak about him, while some jump from the personal to the impersonal form. The words of this psalm remain very much alive today.

O Lord, you search me and you know me,
you know my resting and my rising,

19

you discern my purpose from afar.
You mark when I walk or lie down,
all my ways lie open to you.

Before ever a word is on my tongue
you know it, O Lord, through and through.
Behind and before you besiege me,
your hand ever laid upon me.
Too wonderful for me, this knowledge,
too high, beyond my reach.

O where can I go from your spirit,
or where can I flee from your face?
If I climb the heavens, you are there.
If I lie in the grave, you are there.

If I take the wings of the dawn
and dwell at the sea's furthest end,
even there your hand would lead me,
your right hand would hold me fast.

If I say: 'Let the darkness hide me
and the light around me be night,'
even darkness is not dark for you
and the night is as clear as the day.

This might be summed up colloquially: God always
wins. We may find it hard to be glad at that truth. We may
want to escape from his omniscience and omnipresence.
That cannot be done. So, it is useless for us to become
exasperated and behave like small children, who shut their
eyes and even clench fists against the lids, and then fondly
imagine that they cannot be seen because they themselves
cannot see. However, there seems to be in the psalm a hint
of relief, followed by a smile, because the psalmist has
learned to relax and to welcome the situation. We may try
to do what we like and go where we wish. God does not
merely follow us, for he is already there, and is also with

us, continually loving us. We experience that when we inwardly accept that he is God.

The word 'search' in the first line might make an unfortunate initial impression. It may give the idea of a policeman roughly handling a criminal or a suspect terrorist, or else of an army officer dealing with a prisoner of war. *The Jerusalem Bible* has the word 'examine' instead. Many students would have cause to dislike that word too. Nevertheless, God does necessarily know us better and more deeply than we shall ever know ourselves, with all our needs, desires, inclinations, frustrations, and so on.

That, properly understood, can be a source of strength for us. Why should we be anxious or fearful in our approach to God if he is a friend? When close human friends meet again after a gap of several years, that gap will soon be forgotten if deep down they were loyal and remained mentally, at least, in touch with each other. They could still understand each other despite superficial changes if the friendship had been built on a solid foundation. They might, though, find a need to explain some past happenings to each other, in order to ensure continued acceptance. God never changes. He is always our friend and he always understands fully each one of us and everything affecting us. What a relief never to have to explain anything to him.

In the first part of Psalm 138, the psalmist spoke directly and touchingly to God. Arguing from his own experience to that of all humanity, he expressed wonder at the Lord's omniscience and omnipresence. Now he turns his attention to creation in general and to his own being in particular.

The second part of Psalm 138 starts with the psalmist acknowledging that God was his creator who knew him intimately and all about him from the very moment of his conception and before that time as well. God's prescience is not elaborated as a problem. The psalmist can accept it because of his love and reliance on God. He can even quite simply, and to our minds rather strangely, say that all his future actions were already written in God's book. Another psalm (Ps 55) helps to clarify what is meant by that:

> You have kept an account of my wanderings;
> you have kept a record of my tears;
> are they not written in your book?

The suggestion (which Christ in effect confirmed) is that God is like an unusual accountant who concentrates on the credits and tends to ignore the debits. This is surely an easier way to reach some conclusion with regard to prescience than to enter into bitter arguments about a harmonious relationship between free will and predestination.

The psalmist next admits the seemingly unbridgeable gap which exists between himself and God, whose thoughts are not like his thoughts. As with Isaiah and St Paul, his meditation on God's majesty leads him to wonder and to praise. He concludes with a humble prayer for God to search, test and lead him. Then he will reach eternal life.

> For it was you who created my being,
> knit me together in my mother's womb.
> I thank you for the wonder of my being,
> for the wonders of all your creation.

> Already you knew my soul,
> my body held no secret from you
> when I was being fashioned in secret
> and moulded in the depths of the earth.

> Your eyes saw all my actions,
> they were all of them written in your book;
> every one of my days was decreed
> before one of them came into being.

> To me, how mysterious your thoughts,
> the sum of them not to be numbered!

If I count them, they are more that the sand;
to finish, I must be eternal, like you.

O search me, God, and know my heart.
O test me and know my thoughts.
See that I follow not the wrong path
and lead me in the path of life eternal.

Can this part of the psalm speak to us today? I know an elderly lady whose mother might have miscarried her. In the words of the family doctor at the time, the baby in the womb was 'a fighter', striving not to be delivered into the world prematurely. The risk was great; the mother had had a miscarriage a couple of years before. The lady did not learn about this until her mother told her shortly before her death at an advanced age. Now the daughter says that she can look back on a full life which might not have been, and begin to appreciate with gratitude that God must have wanted her and been concerned for her preservation.

Whatever the circumstances of our own birth may have been, human love working with the God of Love brought each of us into existence. God then sustained us, and he will ensure our survival throughout the span of our earthly life. Some words of Cardinal Newman might be applied here:

God has created me to do him some definite service; he has committed some work to me which he has not committed to another... Therefore I will trust him.

All of this is mysterious, culminating with God's promise of eternal life if we follow his path. Still more mysterious is the thought that God the Son became part of creation, a baby in Mary's womb, and that he was born, lived and died. It is he who can lead us on the way to eternal life.

4

God's love

By studying a map of England it is possible to guess why many towns grew up where they did. Some, for reasons of communication and trade, are situated at the junction of natural land routes or of rivers. Some were developed when a source of wealth such as coal was discovered; the name can indicate that. Others, on the borders or the coastline, were needed to protect the adjoining areas and their inhabitants, and so were heavily fortified.

With all our different and even conflicting emotions, feelings and talents, each of us might resemble a town. There can seem to be many voices inside us, but one or another predominates from time to time. I am now particularly thinking of occasions when we may feel like a besieged city. Life seems to want to batter us down. Then it is easy to respond with a mental drawing up of the drawbridge and a shrinking into ourselves. Others seem to threaten us or they might provoke us; but by going inwards in fear we would find ourselves confronted with our personal limitations.

Self-defence is a fundamental principle. However, is a narrowing in life the best and only solution? An indication that that may be happening, I suggest, is when we become aware of how much we are silently talking to ourselves. Without realising it, we in fact spend a considerable amount of time each day in doing that. The danger is that we may become too self-absorbed, if we are reluctant to converse with other people.

A way out of this impasse is to tell ourselves to thank and praise God. Psalm 102 might be very helpful to us:

My soul, give thanks to the Lord,
all my being, bless his holy name.
My soul, give thanks to the Lord
and never forget all his blessings.

It is he who forgives all your guilt,
who heals every one of your ills,
who redeems your life from the grave,
who crowns you with love and compassion,
who fills your life with good things...

The Lord is compassion and love,
slow to anger and rich in mercy.
His wrath will come to an end;
he will not be angry for ever.
He does not treat us according to our sins
nor repay us according to our faults.

For as the heavens are high above the earth
so strong is his love for those who fear him.
As far as the east is from the west
so far does he remove our sins.

As a father has compassion on his sons,
the Lord has pity on those who fear him;
for he knows of what we are made.
he remembers that we are dust.

As for man, his days are like grass;
he flowers like the flower of the field;
the wind blows and he is gone
and his place never sees him again.

But the love of the Lord is everlasting
upon those who hold him in fear;
his justice reaches out to children's children
when they keep his covenant in truth,
when they keep his will in their mind.

The Lord has set his sway in heaven
and his kingdom is ruling over all.
Give thanks to the Lord, all his angels,
mighty in power, fulfilling his word,
who heed the voice of his word.

Give thanks to the Lord, all his hosts,
his servants who do his will.
Give thanks to the Lord, all his works,
in every place where he rules.
My soul, give thanks to the Lord!

The psalmist has an expansive view of life. He has the insight to say, in effect, that God has not only reversed the effects of original sin (which were sin, suffering and death) but that he has also crowned and filled us with goodness. That recalls Mary and her *Magnificat* (see Ch. 1), as does the climax, that God's love is ageless, upon those who respect him. Those heartening words are addressed to us too.

Just as Mary may have had this psalm in her mind, so the psalmist may have consciously included some references to the Old Testament. The beginning of the character-sketch of God resembles the words he said to Moses on the mountain of Sinai (Ex 34:6):

The Lord, the Lord, a God of tenderness and
    compassion,
slow to anger, rich in kindness and faithfulness.

Paul would, much later, tell the Romans (5:20) that 'however great the number of sins committed, grace was even greater.'

Further, some texts from the Book of Isaiah (55:9; 38:17; 40:6-8) may have provided sources for later verses in the psalm:

1. Yes, the heavens are as high above earth
   as my ways are above your ways,
   my thoughts above your thoughts.

26

2. You have thrust all my sins
   behind your back.

3. All flesh is grass
   and its beauty like the wild flower's.
   The grass withers, the flower fades
   when the breath of the Lord blows on them...
   but the word of our God remains for ever.

A striking difference between the psalm and the first text is that the height of heaven is stated by the psalm not to indicate God's distance from us, but instead the strength of his love for us. Similarly, he does not merely turn his back on our sins; he removes them to the furthest horizon. We know that his own Son did that for us. Although it is unpleasant for us on Ash Wednesday to be reminded that we are dust, God remembers that to our advantage. Very touching, too, is the development of the third text. We are frail and passing; but the psalm holds out a promise that, when we respect God, his everlasting love will raise us up. Jesus himself went further and used the image of grass and flowers very meaningfully (Mt 6:28-34). Flowers are robed more wonderfully than King Solomon was; yet they are thrown out and burnt. Human beings are of more value than flowers. So, we are not to worry. God knows what we need and he cares for us. If we have our priorities right, and put his kingdom first, 'all these other things' will be ours as well.

The psalm ends with a three-fold call on creation, angels and saints, to thank God, emphasising the need to follow him and his wishes. There follow, but with a deeper significance, the initial words:

My soul, give thanks to the Lord!

May my innermost being always be a place where God rules. Then external conflicts will not really disturb my peace.

5

God as judge

When I had made a few preliminary points, the Old Bailey judge questioned me about my background and my career. As I replied, he studied my face closely, sympathetically and with interest. He often took time to respond, instinctively wishing to be certain, I suppose, that he correctly understood my words, and then wanting to weigh up how to proceed. He was an expert in eliciting information, but I did not feel at all threatened. I was not, however, a criminal in the dock, being judged by him. We were in my small editorial office, and I was helping him with the script for a new edition of his book.

The experience of such a meeting was, of course, memorable; he showed such individual concern for me. This helps to explain why I feel happy at the prospect of the Last Judgment. God is love, and he is infinitely true and wise. He wants each of us to be saved, and so his own dear Son came on earth to redeem us. He would never want us to blame ourselves unnecessarily. He would encourage us, and welcome and accept the smallest signs of repentance. He sees the good in us, which he himself has implanted there. He is not like a human stickler for justice. He brings in equity and fairness, as we learn when we try to live by the basic two-fold law of love of him and of neighbour.

The Jews could enthuse because God was their king and ruler, as well as being the creator, king and judge of the whole world. As Psalm 95 begins:

O sing a new song to the Lord,
sing to the Lord all the earth.
O sing to the Lord, bless his name.

Proclaim his help day by day,
tell among the nations his glory
and his wonders among all the peoples.

God not only created the heavens, sea and land in the beginning. He continues to sustain them each day, and he continues to save his people day by day too. In contrast to him and his power, the heathens' gods are obviously nothing. He is majestic and splendid.

An appeal is made to the families of peoples to give to the Lord the glory which is his due. They are even invited to bring offerings and worship him in his temple. He, in turn, will judge them fairly.

The psalmist then turns to the divisions of creation and, personifying them, invites them each to praise God:

Let the heavens rejoice and earth be glad,
let the sea and all within it thunder praise,
let the land and all it bears rejoice,
all the trees of the wood shout for joy

at the presence of the Lord for he comes,
he comes to rule the earth.
With justice he will rule the world,
he will judge the peoples with his truth.

Rex tremendae maiestatis: those words from the *Dies irae* in Verdi's *Requiem* can thrill us and make us tremble, but they are followed by calmer thoughts, a request to Jesus to recall that it was for our sake that he became man and sought us, even to suffering the cross. He forgave Mary Magdalen and the penitent thief. So surely we can have hope as well and, co-operating with him, we shall eventually reach his eternal rest.

6

God – desire for him

From November 1987 for some while, an exhibition was held in Westminster Cathedral devoted to the eighty-five martyrs of England and Wales. On 22 November, Pope John Paul II had beatified those men who had suffered and died in the sixteenth and seventeenth centuries.

I never failed to be moved by one photograph in particular. It was of a part of the cell in the Tower of London where a young priest, Fr George Beesley, was confined, alone, in 1590. He was then aged 27 and had been working in England for only two years before his arrest. The notorious Richard Topcliffe had him tortured so severely that friends could hardly recognise him. Nevertheless, in 1590, as the picture showed, he scratched on the wall of his cell in Latin the opening words of Psalm 41 (see Ch. 15):

Like the deer that yearns
for running streams,
so my soul is yearning
for you, my God.

That was a firm, impassioned expression of faith, hope and love in extremely grim circumstances. He was put to death in the next year. For him, God's love was better than this life.

It is unlikely that any of us will be called upon to give up our freedom and life in this way. We may, though, have an accident or become ill, and so be confined to bed for a while. Possibly, the illness could be mental rather than physical. Alternatively, we may be asked to undertake work which we dislike or which we feel is using only a fraction of our potential. These are examples of temporary losses of some physical, mental or emotional freedom. Fr Beesley had all three combined in a worse manner, because he was imprisoned for an indefinite period, in a solitary cell; was innocent of any crime; had no means of seeking a remedy; and so faced death. Despite all this, for him it resulted in a great development and upsurgence in his spiritual life. When he carved out those Latin words from the wall, he may have done so to sustain himself and to keep off despair. Then, they would have become an inspiration to him.

When we are led by the Holy Spirit, we too are capable of great things; but we must be led by God, not by our own inclinations. God, not money, status or power, must really be our God; and the test can come when any of those other things are taken, even partially or temporarily, from us. We were made for God, and we shall find no rest until we rest in him. Our present life is a pilgrimage, but Christ goes with and before us. He helps us to carry our troubles and sufferings, if we look to him frequently for assistance. God is love, and he does not want our relationship with him to be solely one of dependence. He wants us to return love to him.

These are some ideas which come to me when reading a favourite psalm (Ps 62). It is used on many feast days as the first psalm in the Morning Prayer of the Church:

O God, you are my God, for you I long;
for you my soul is thirsting.
My body pines for you
like a dry, weary land without water.
So I gaze on you in the sanctuary
to see your strength and your glory.

For your love is better than life,
my lips will speak your praise.
So I will bless you all my life,
in your name I will lift up my hands.
My soul shall be filled as with a bouquet,
my mouth shall provide you with joy.

On my bed I remember you.
On you I muse through the night
for you have been my help;
in the shadow of your wings I rejoice.
My soul clings to you;
your right hand holds me fast.

This psalm is about thirsting for God with all of one's being. He is my Lord and my God, as many of us pray at the consecration in the Mass. He gave each of us life, so that we may live with him and not for ourselves. He has always been, and will continue to be, our help.

Taken literally, this psalm has helped me. When faced with a problem, I tend to have broken nights. I found that an ideal way to prevent mental turmoil, or uncharitable thoughts, overwhelming me during the small hours of the night, was to pray a psalm (and often, Psalm 62) very slowly from memory. I would then be able to turn all my thoughts gently to God, putting the problem in his hands, and so become relaxed. I had mistaken 'the shadow' of God's 'wings' as a problem when, viewed properly and using words from Francis Thompson's *The Hound of Heaven*, my gloom was, after all, the shade of God's hand, outstretched caressingly. The psalm goes even further: God's 'right hand holds me fast'.

7

God's protection

At night-time during the last war, my brothers and I always went upstairs to sleep in our beds. Unlike our neighbours, we did not have a reinforced, though damp, garage, or any other kind of air-raid shelter; and the German pilots of the bombers droning overhead were more intent on paralysing inner London than our suburb.

Occasionally, however, we had to put up with the noise, vibrations and fears of an attack, say on the anti-aircraft battery situated about a mile to the South. Even then, our reaction in the morning was to go out early collecting shrapnel, jagged pieces of metal which had fallen from the sky. It did not occur to us children that each piece could have killed someone.

We lived outside the area for compulsory evacuation, and our parents did not know anyone prepared to take in a large young family. By staying where we were, our education continued without interruption, and we remained together. Our father's office was quite close, too. He would gleefully tell visitors to our home that we need not get worried until a bomb came labelled with our address. There never was such a bomb, and after 1945 the amount of the house's war damage repairs claim was trivial.

It would not have been appropriate for every family in England to have taken the same stance as our parents. Nevertheless, as believers in God we can all be assured that, when we weigh up a difficult situation prayerfully, try to act as we are led to believe he wishes, and try to trust in him, he will protect us in a special way. Psalm 90 deals with the effects in our lives of this attitude. Unfortunately, it is too long for all of it to be printed here, and I am omitting the central portion:

He who dwells in the shelter of the Most High
and abides in the shade of the Almighty
says to the Lord: 'My refuge,
my stronghold, my God in whom I trust!'

It is he who will free you from the snare
of the fowler who seeks to destroy you;
he will conceal you with his pinions
and under his wings you will find refuge.

You will not fear the terror of the night
nor the arrow that flies by day,
nor the plague that prowls in the darkness
nor the scourge that lays waste at noon...

Since he clings to me in love, I will free him;
protect him, for he knows my name.
When he calls I shall answer: 'I am with you.'
I will save him in distress and give him glory.

With length of life I will content him;
I shall let him see my saving power.

In the last verses, God is supposed to be speaking; while in this translation the psalm started impersonally but then became personal, directed to the listener or reader. Such changes are not unusual in the psalms. They can help to enliven the words and aid meditation.

Thomas More, imprisoned in the Tower of London in 1534, found that. As he told his daughter Meg in a letter, he had already suffered many agonies with his heavy fearful heart, forecasting all such perils and painful deaths as might happen to him. In an attempt to control and direct his imagination and his natural tendency to shrink from pain and death, he spent time in praying and writing.

One book of his from this period, *The Dialogue of Comfort against Tribulation*, contains a lengthy commentary on Psalm 90. It reads rather like a lawyer's argument for his client with some humorous stories thrown in. The underlying intent, though, is grim: to seek God's strength and to conform his will to God's should he be brought to the peril of martyrdom. Here is a brief account of the commentary.

Fighting any temptation is painful, but when we are under God's wings and protected by him, 'merry in remembrance of his mercy', no power can pull us out against our will. In the night, a danger can steal on us unawares. Those lacking faith can overreact, and almost provoke an attack on themselves. 'Sometimes the thing that on the sea seemeth a rock is indeed nothing else but a mist.' The arrow of the day means pride in worldly prosperity. The darkness means the hours before dawn, before grace has given out a full light, or evening, when grace may be departing. Those in such conditions hardly know the way or where to go, because they are set on pleasure which draws them into sin, or on the wish to heap up possessions. The scourge at noon is plain open persecution, an attempt to drive a person to give up his faith. This, the saint maintained, is the most perilous of the four temptations. Despite, that, if we took to heart that our Saviour gave up everything for us sinners, we might be content in return to give up all that God has lent to us for our use in this life rather than forsake him. Thomas More then tried to face his fear of a shameful and painful death by imagining in some detail Christ's bitter painful passion, hoping to 'inflame our key-cold hearts, and set them on fire with his love'. For our suffering, God will 'highly reward us with everlasting wealth... If we die here for him, we shall in heaven everlastingly both live and also reign with him!'

8

God's ways (1)

'I can see lots of fluffy cottonwool.' 'And I can see lots and lots of fluffy bunny rabbits.' 'I can see a pterodactyl.' 'And I can see the British Isles.' 'Come along, children, and stop staring at the clouds or you'll all fall over.'

Adults, too, can interpret nature in various ways. A farmer, a property developer and a rambler standing at the edge of the same cornfield may each regard it quite differently. This applies to the witness of our other senses as well.

When adults, or children, try to interpret each other, far more complications arise. We do not often know all the relevant facts, but may think that we do. We may over-use our imaginations, be unaware of the background and misunderstand the meaning of the events. We may be, ignorantly, the victims of prejudice. It is almost impossible for us to look at life objectively, for we are involved in it and have what we regard as our own place in it, which we try to protect. We are influenced by our inheritance, background, education, relationships, social and economic conditions, physical and mental powers and limitations, our expectations, and so on. We are creatures, but we can try to behave like gods. We do not really understand ourselves, let alone others.

Should humans wish to interpret God's ways, it would be advisable to bear in mind words of Paul (and of the prophet Isaiah quoted by him) in his Letter to the Romans (11:33-34):

How deep are (God's) wisdom and knowledge! Who can explain his decisions? Who can understand his ways? As the scripture says, 'Who knows the mind of the Lord? Who is able to give him advice?'

Nevertheless, we may be able to sympathise with the psalmist who protested:

I said: 'This is what causes my grief;
that the way of the Most High has changed.'

His interpretation was defective, but at least he had stopped complaining in general and had pinpointed what he thought was the fundamental trouble. He may have been a priest, speaking for the people of Israel, and he may be referring later to the priestly custom of spending a night in the Temple.

Psalm 76 begins with a lament:

I cry aloud to God,
cry aloud to God that he may hear me.

Such desperation may come to each of us individually at some time. Silent prayer seems impossible, if not useless. We must, as it were, besiege God, who seems to be shut away in his heaven. Our need can appear to us to be more important than what concerns him. He must attend to us quickly. The psalmist proceeds to detail, almost queru-lously, the complaints which he imagines he has against God. He has raised his hands ceaselessly at night (perhaps in the Temple), but he could not really pray. God withheld sleep from him, but he spent the time in (futile) question-ing. He would not be consoled. Would the Lord reject Israel completely? Had he ended his promise? More touch-ingly, was he forgetting his mercy and in anger withhold-ing his compassion?

The belief and knowledge that God is merciful and compassionate may have been what influenced the psalm-ist. Although he next articulates his central problem, that God's way has seemingly changed, he is ready to argue on from it. He thinks of God's past, wonderful dealings with his people:

I muse on all your works
and ponder your mighty deeds.

He takes time to do that, and some sense of balance and perspective returns. He can then make an act of faith:

Your ways, O God, are holy.
What god is great as our God?

Truly, God does work wonders and he has shown his power by saving his people. Similarly, when we each examine our own lives, we shall surely find examples of God's great works, starting with our very existence and birth and our baptism.

Unless, as is possible, the verses come from an earlier psalm, the psalmist's memory and tongue are now loosened. He revels in a poetic account of the crossing of the Red Sea. Then his tone becomes simple, hushed and factual as he surrenders to God by concluding:

You guided your people like a flock
by the hand of Moses and Aaron.

Many people today do not like what they see as God's ways. Why does he allow the innocent to suffer? Why did he not intervene to prevent the horrors of the gas chambers and the concentration camps? Why do small children die from cancer? The questions are many. Could we understand the answers? In any event, is God, the Supreme Being, answerable to us?

Christ, Son of the Most High, proclaimed that he is the way, yet he himself was changed in appearance by his sufferings and cruel death. As Isaiah wrote (53:2-5):

Without beauty, without majesty (we saw him),
no looks to attract our eyes;
a thing despised and rejected by men,
a man of sorrows and familiar with suffering,

a man to make people screen their faces;
he was despised and we took no account of him.

And yet ours were the sufferings he bore,
ours the sorrows he carried.
But we, we thought of him as someone punished,
struck by God, and brought low...
On him lies a punishment that brings us peace,
and through his wounds we are healed.

Out of Christ's superficial defeat came a glorious victory for him and for us – the resurrection.

God has a way for each one of us as well. In the early Church, Christianity was named 'the Way', and our calling is still to try to imitate our Leader. Circumstances may suddenly change for us, from health to sickness, prosperity to unemployment, a happy relationship to bereavement. Detailed questioning of God will not help us. His ways are beyond our full understanding. We have to trust him, for his ways are holy.

9

God's ways (2)

Does your Confirmation patron saint mean a lot to you? A relation of mine, when confirmed as a young boy, chose Augustine, because that was the longest name he knew. Later in life, he had the opportunity to study the saint's writings, and he could then appreciate them and his choice of patron.

My Confirmation saint is Thérèse of Lisieux, and I often think of her when coming to the end of Psalm 112. Like Psalm 115 (see Ch. 41) Psalm 112 would have been sung by Christ and the apostles on the first Maundy Thursday evening. Like Psalm 147 (see Ch. 2) the Church makes frequent use of it in the Office; sometimes Psalm 147 is recited immediately after it.

> Praise, O servants of the Lord,
> praise the name of the Lord!
> May the name of the Lord be blessed
> both now and for evermore!
> From the rising of the sun to its setting
> praised be the name of the Lord!
>
> High above all nations is the Lord,
> above the heavens his glory.
> Who is like the Lord, our God,
> who has risen on high to his throne
> yet stoops from the heights to look down,
> to look down upon heaven and earth?
>
> From the dust he lifts up the lowly,
> from his misery he raises the poor
> to set him in the company of princes,

yes, with the princes of his people.
To the childless wife he gives a home
and gladdens her heart with children.

The first group of verses contains praise, three times, for the name of the Lord. All his servants, who include the followers of Christ, are to join in. The phrase about the rising and setting of the sun might mean East and West, so that God is praised, not only in all times, but also in all places. The words recall, too, a frequently used Eucharistic Prayer.

The next group of verses at first portrays God in his majesty and power, as a distant ruler. The emphasis is then completely and movingly changed. It is as though the psalmist suddenly, in his love for God, became irritated at being confined to a formal type of prayer. God is not aloof. There is no one like him. He behaves in a way that could hardly have been anticipated. Although he is supreme, he remains concerned for his creation. Pictures of him decorating mediaeval manuscripts come to mind: at the top, left-hand corner of the sheet, in an initial letter, possibly for the start of this psalm, there is a benevolent-looking old man, leaning over the parapet of a stone tower and gazing downwards, while at the bottom of the page some people are drawn. Among them, lords and ladies are obvious, in their rich clothes, as are priests and nuns in their habits. There are also labourers holding various tools and peasant women with children. God looks down on earth, enabling people to look up to him.

What does God see? He notices those in need of his mercy and care. That, in fact, means each and every person, including you and me. The psalmist, though, singles out those whom Jewish society, and our own today, might easily tend to reject: the humble, when self-assertion is stressed; the poor, when prosperity is regarded as a sign of God's favour; the childless wife, when her husband longs to perpetuate his name and family.

It is the saints, servants of the Lord, who, as a result of

41

prayer and a close co-operation with God, can learn how he reacts. They are people who have turned to God and have tried to let their thoughts be so influenced by his thoughts that their ways come to resemble his ways. We can think of Mary. In her *Magnificat* (see Ch. 1) she showed not only that she was fully aware of God's reversal of ordinary, accepted human values, but also that she was not insecure and afraid as a result. She could revel in the marvel of his works.

Thérèse, just a century ago and not very long after her entry into the Carmelite convent, expressed her desire to be the kind of person that Jesus would notice. So she wrote to her sister that she wanted to be like a grain of sand, always in its place, beneath everyone's feet, and ignored by all except for Jesus. Her writing was not the raving of a lunatic; she was a calm, self-possessed person. It was the overflowing poetic exaggeration of a great lover of God. She always tried to live simply and, on her deathbed, could rejoice that she had always remained working in the convent's novitiate. A lay-sister had asked in her hearing: 'What can we say about Sister Thérèse when she is dead?' Immediately after her death, she asked Thérèse for forgiveness, and was cured of a long-term illness.

The endorsement by the Church of Thérèse's Little Way of trust and absolute self-surrender confirms that she reached a deep understanding of God's ways towards us. A childlike trust in him enabled her to be strongly aware of his mercy, and to see that he likes us to throw ourselves into his arms. He then can, and will, raise us up.

10

God as shepherd

Is there any point, I wondered, in trying to write about 'The Lord is my shepherd'? Psalm 22 (Psalm 23 in the Hebrew numbering system) is so well known and very much loved. Poets have rewritten it in verse and composers have set it to music. I shied away from it; but recently, in times of relaxation, its words kept coming into my mind.

Although unfortunately our familiarity with it may have made the psalm seem rather hackneyed, it is not a mere cosy, comfortable, pretty piece of writing. Contrasted with Psalm 62 (see Ch. 6) it certainly lacks the dramatic force of passion. Instead, it is calm, but firm, positive and dignified:

> The Lord is my shepherd;
> there is nothing I shall want.
> Fresh and green are the pastures
> where he gives me repose.
> Near restful waters he leads me,
> to revive my drooping spirit.
>
> He guides me along the right path;
> he is true to his name.
> If I should walk in the valley of darkness
> no evil would I fear.
> You are there with your crook and your staff;
> with these you give me comfort.
>
> You have prepared a banquet for me
> in the sight of my foes.
> My head you have anointed with oil;
> my cup is overflowing.

Surely goodness and kindness shall follow me
all the days of my life.
In the Lord's own house shall I dwell
for ever and ever.

It occurred to me that the first two lines may contain a key to an interpretation. The Lord is looking after the psalmist and is giving him everything that he wants. What is God said to be doing and giving? He gives nutritious and suitable food, with water and even wine to drink. He provides facilities for rest, washing and the recovery of strength in lovely surroundings. He leads and he guides. He ensures that harm is avoided even when close, and he is also prepared, if necessary, to take action. He will rescue the lost with his crook and threaten thieves or batter down thorns with his staff. The imagery suddenly changes, and he has become the generous host at a banquet who himself carries out the good work of anointing his guest's head with oil.

All of that can easily be applied to ordinary material requirements for human life. The psalmist may have been passing in review his experience over a long life. As Christians we can also apply the words to spiritual gifts and activities, to the sacraments and to the Church.

What, on the other hand, did God seek from the psalmist? How can he so confidently expect life for ever in God's very own house? Answers to those questions are not supplied, but seem to be there by implication.

Like us, the psalmist no doubt had to learn by the hard way through making mistakes. There was almost certainly a time when the Lord was not genuinely his shepherd, when he was attracted by what might be called the fluorescent green of some plastic, imitation grass. He would have been ruled by pride and self-love. Now, however, it is obvious that something happened, even over a long period, and that he has become fully committed to God. He wishes what God wishes and God's plans for him are accepted as if they were his plans for himself. There is no longer a tension between himself and God, but instead harmony. He has directed his will and love away from self and towards God. He is living as nearly as possible as humanity was intended to live.

It is amazing and wonderful that the creator treats each one of us as an individual person and with respect. He does not force us, although he may strongly and clearly offer to lead us. He presents each one of us throughout our lives with numerous choices of varying importance. Whenever we fail, he gives us more chances. If our key decisions, at least, are made with him in mind and with the wish not to offend him, then we shall gradually fulfil our destiny with his help. He enlists our co-operation throughout. There are times when he wishes us to be active; there are also periods when he expects us to be almost passive in his hands, for we have to learn in practice that we are dependent upon him. This can be painful, but when we have come through we shall see that the work was really his. All that we had to do was to accept him, turn fully towards him, and trust and love him. He gives and he does all the rest.

11

Creation (1)

'O Lord, how wonderful!' The words escaped from my lips although I was alone, driving my car on an unfamiliar country road in England. The route had been uphill and tree-lined, but the car had just come round a bend. Without a map-reader sitting beside me, I had not known what to expect. Trees no longer confined my view. Before and below me lay a wide expanse of fields and hedgerows, stretching to distant hills of hazy blue under a bright sky.

My exclamation was, I think, a form of praise of God for his creation and for his gift of life. However, much of what I saw had not been, even figuratively speaking, arranged by him. Over thousands of years our original countryside has been changed and shaped by human activity. Nevertheless, the scene struck me with its beauty and majesty, an example of how God blesses such striving.

Visitors are drawn to London by its historic buildings. Some also marvel at humbler things. Children are talented at that. Once I saw a child in a pushchair point out to her mother a brass letterbox set in the wall near an office door, and try to keep gazing back at it after the family had unheedingly moved on. Adults can be blasé, but children are discovering the world. We would do well, though, to learn their uncomplicated, trusting approach to God.

One of the first psalms in the Psalter, Psalm 8, brought these ideas to my mind. Rather like a good sonnet in modern literature, it is beautifully and compactly written. It begins with praise of God who is great throughout the earth. While angels above the heavens glorify him directly, even human children can praise him. The creator and the created are then contrasted. God made and arranged the heavens; yet amazingly he thinks of us and looks after us.

He loves us. In his enthusiasm, the psalmist declares that God gives us such power and honour that we are almost godlike, and he cannot resist indicating the kinds of life (in the three regions of earth, air and water) which are subject to human control. The initial praise of God is repeated, this time with a strong undertone of thanksgiving and love:

> How great is your name, O Lord our God,
> through all the earth!
>
> Your majesty is praised above the heavens;
> on the lips of children and of babes
> you have found praise to foil your enemy,
> to silence the foe and the rebel.
>
> When I see the heavens, the work of your hands,
> the moon and the stars which you arranged,
> what is man that you should keep him in mind,
> mortal man that you care for him?
>
> Yet you have made him little less than a god;
> with glory and honour you crowned him,
> gave him power over the works of your hand,
> put all things under his feet.
>
> All of them, sheep and cattle,
> yes, even the savage beasts,
> birds of the air, and fish
> that make their way through the waters.
>
> How great is your name, O Lord our God,
> through all the earth!

Living at the end of the twentieth century, we are conscious that we are only the stewards or trustees, as it were, not the masters or owners, of creation. We are to use it, not exploit it. We are to accept some responsibility for the welfare of all living creatures, whose habitats can be drastically altered or lost by our activity. Just as we look after the material world, so the creator looks after us. The psalmist disparagingly asked God: 'What is man?' At the appointed time, God gave his answer by sending his Son who was born of Mary. Pope St Leo the Great could say in the fifth century when preaching at Christmas: 'O Christian, be aware of your nobility – it is God's own nature that you share.'

This psalm can also be read in relation to Christ. He is not godlike; he is God and the Man. As God he created and arranged the heavens. St Paul wrote (Col 1:17):

> All things were created
> through him and for him.
> He is before all things
> and in him all things hold together.

Following his death and resurrection, he is the reconciler of all to the Father so that, as Paul further wrote, God's plan might be fulfilled, to unite in Christ 'everything in heaven and everything on earth' (Eph 1:10).

You and I are caught up in this. We are in Christ by being members of his Church. We are not only called by his name, Christians, but we are also, in some manner, other Christs. God always keeps each one of us in mind. He loves each of us as he loves his own Son. We can look forward confidently to the time when he will be all in all.

12

Creation (2)

In a half awake state, I let the escalator carry me up towards the surface. This was like the end of any morning's journey to work, but I suddenly became aware of the harsh, grating noise made by the escalator as it staggered upwards. Then I noticed how I was surrounded and almost shut in by things made by man, especially from metal and concrete. I felt alienated. All of this was lifeless. As a recompense, I would soon be walking to a leafy London square.

Thinking about the beauties and wonders of God's creation can encourage us; rejoicing in it with him is better still. Psalm 103 may help us to do that. It reveals a childlike delight in the world and its various parts as seen many hundreds of years ago:

Bless the Lord, my soul!
Lord God, how great you are,
clothed in majesty and glory,
wrapped in light as in a robe!

The psalmist begins by calling on himself to praise God. He introduces beautiful images of the Lord clothed in majesty and enrobed in light. According to Genesis, God created light on the first day (1:3-5). Jesus said that he was the light of the world and the light of life (Jn 8:12), and so for Christians light, often from candles, has a special significance.

The psalm is a meditation on the creation story with some embellishments. God's dwelling is above the rains which fall from heaven. The heavens themselves are stretched out like a tent over the whole of creation. The natural forces of wind and lightning serve God. First it is stated that he established a fixed earth, which he wrapped 'with the ocean like a cloak'. Then an account is given of how the towering, chaotic waters were checked and subdued, so that they flowed where directed. Life-giving springs gushed in valleys instead. There is a nice description of beasts and wild asses drinking, while birds sing from trees on the banks.

Hinting at the complex interdependence of the world, the psalmist considers how the wet earth produces grass on which cattle feed, and plants for man. He makes bread, wine and oil to strengthen and cheer himself. The trees need water, too. Birds can nest on them, even on the cedars of Lebanon. On the theme of homes, the psalmist mentions the stork on a tree-top, goats on mountains and rabbits in rocks. All has its place – but, as Jesus was to say, 'the Son of Man has nowhere to lay his head' (Mt 8:20).

Carrying on with the story of creation, reference is made to the moon and the sun. Night-time is for the beasts:

The young lions roar for their prey
and ask their food from God.

The psalmist does not seem to be upset by what lions eat, but his thought recalls the idea of drinking birds giving thanks to God when they pause, raise their heads and swallow. At dawn, the wild animals retire:

Man goes forth to his work,
to labour till evening falls.

At this point, the psalmist enthuses:

How many are your works, O Lord!
In wisdom you have made them all.
The earth is full of your riches.

Even so, he was unaware of riches deep in the earth, such as mineral wealth. Then he thinks of the sea, vast,

wide and somewhat threatening. He sums up the situation
for all creatures:

All of these look to you
to give them their food in due season.
You give it, they gather it up:
you open your hand, they have their fill.

You hide your face, they are dismayed;
you take back your spirit, they die,
returning to the dust from which they came.
You send forth your spirit, they are created;
and you renew the face of the earth.

That last verse may well be familiar to you, for it is
often used in prayer to the Holy Spirit. The psalmist continues with praise to God for his works and his power:

He looks on the earth and it trembles:
the mountains send forth smoke at his touch.

Despite the awesome signs of earthquakes and volcanic
eruptions, the psalmist is so confident in God's goodness
that he is not troubled:

I will sing to the Lord all my life,
make music to my God while I live.

He can even express the wish:

May my thoughts be pleasing to him.
I find my joy in the Lord.

He allows himself a mild outburst against the existence
of the wicked, but he ends as he began:

Bless the Lord, my soul.

13

Creation (3)

Perhaps it is a common reaction, but I found that, when I joined a firm, I somehow imagined that the organisation had always been, and would always remain, as it then was. That may have revealed an unexpressed need for security. On the other hand, when I left that firm I noticed, as an outsider, how quickly changes came about, whether in personnel, systems or office location.

The writer of Psalm 145 was fully aware of the transience of human life. I used to read his words as relating to those who planned fraud or other deceits. However, the verses need not be so limited:

> Put no trust in princes,
> in mortal men in whom there is no help.
> Take their breath, they return to clay
> and their plans that day come to nothing.

This is a down-to-earth, realistic assessment of our human predicament. We cannot be certain from day to day, even from minute to minute, about what may or will happen to us. For Christians, that is not a cause for fear, but for trust in the Lord.

The psalmist began with an invitation to himself to praise God, and he happily replies to that:

> My soul, give praise to the Lord;
> I will praise the Lord all my days,
> make music to my God while I live.

After his brief but penetrating look at humanity, he

turns his thoughts again to God, with praise and wonder, and in strongly contrasting words:

He is happy who is helped by Jacob's God,
whose hope is in the Lord his God,
who alone made heaven and earth,
the seas and all they contain.

It is he who keeps faith for ever,
who is just to those who are oppressed.
It is he who gives bread to the hungry,
the Lord, who sets prisoners free,

the Lord who gives sight to the blind,
who raises up those who are bowed down,
the Lord, who protects the stranger
and upholds the widow and orphan.

It is the Lord who loves the just
but thwarts the path of the wicked.
The Lord will reign for ever,
Sion's God, from age to age.

It is hard to make our own the truth that God who made each and every part of creation, attends to us and our needs. Normally, he does that through the instrumentality of other human beings. God would never make a promise to us in vain, and being almighty and eternal he can and will fulfil his promises. One of the most important of those for us is found in Christ's parting words to his disciples before his ascension: 'Know that I am with you always; yes, to the end of time' (Mt 28:20). He is with each of us as individuals, and also with us as his Church.

The psalm contains tangible examples of how God can free us from physical oppression, such as hunger, imprisonment or blindness. At the start of his public ministry, Jesus would quote similar words from the prophet Isaiah, and he made a great impression on all who listened to him in the synagogue (Lk 4:18-22). What he said and how he said it, promising a fulfilment of the text, answered a deeply felt need. He gave encouragement and hope.

Despite superficial appearances, God does continue to care for and protect his creation. We cannot understand that unless we accept that he is God and that he is in ultimate control both now and for ever.

14

Creation (4)

Adults can find it hard to accept that God enjoys his creation. We see and experience so much seemingly unjustified suffering and oppression. How can the Supreme Being care when he does not intervene to prevent such occurrences? Children may have a happier reaction to life. When they like doing something, such as building with bricks, then a child brought up in a Christian home may conclude that God too likes playing with bricks in heaven; for if there were no bricks in heaven to play with, how could a child be happy there?

The writer of Psalm 146 seems to have had a childlike, innocent and unsophisticated view of life. He begins by praising God, and refers to the restoration of Israel by the rebuilding of Jerusalem, the city, and the return of the exiled people. For them, God provides healing and he binds up their wounds. There is a strange transition. God, as creator, fixes the number and names of the stars. He has control of them. That contrast between his dealings with individual humans and those affecting the material universe, may be quaintly worded to our minds, but it strikingly indicates God's mastery. The stars are his playthings.

God's greatness and wisdom are asserted. However, as other psalms and as Mary in the *Magnificat* (see Ch. 1) also declared, his values can be the reverse of ours. He raises and lowers where humans would tend to do the opposite. The psalmist turns his attention to some examples of God's detailed care for creation. In language recalling that of Psalm 103 (see Ch. 12) he gives a picture of a bare mountainside becoming covered with grass and plants, which provide food for humans, animals and birds.

The last two verses contain a superficially charming but

nevertheless shrewd view of what pleases God. It was a breakthrough for humanity when the horse was tamed and could be ridden. Men on horseback had superior height, speed and power to those on the ground. The use of horses facilitated travel and the migration of peoples. God, though, is not delighted merely in horses and human prowess. Other psalms contain similar thoughts. Thus, Psalm 32 says:

> A king is not saved by his army,
> nor a warrior preserved by his strength.
> A vain hope for safety is the horse;
> despite its power it cannot save.

God alone is our Saviour. So in our age we could say that it is useless to put our total trust in weapons of war, although some deterrent strength is needed. Psalm 32 continues:

> The Lord looks on those who revere him,
> on those who hope in his love.

It expands on this theme, whereas the ending of Psalm 146 is more forceful and concise. When we believe that God is love, waiting for his love may seem strange; but life proves the necessity of that for us. God must test us, and he is the Lord of time. He himself does not need any kind of testing by us. Paul would write to the Romans: 'As if God meant to prove how well he loves us, it was while we were still sinners that Christ, in his own appointed time, died for us' (5:8). It is for us, co-operating with offered grace, to reach out and accept God's love at his appointed time, knowing that he has, in fact, loved us from before the foundation of the world.

> Praise the Lord for he is good;
> sing to our God for he is loving;
> to him our praise is due.

The Lord builds up Jerusalem
and brings back Israel's exiles,
he heals the broken-hearted,
he binds up all their wounds.
He fixes the number of the stars;
he calls each one by its name.

Our Lord is great and almighty;
his wisdom can never be measured.
The Lord raises the lowly;
he humbles the wicked to the dust.
O sing to the Lord, giving thanks;
sing psalms to our God with the harp.

He covers the heavens with clouds;
he prepares the rain for the earth,
making mountains sprout with grass
and with plants to serve man's needs.
He provides the beasts with their food
and young ravens that call upon him.

His delight is not in horses
nor his pleasure in warriors' strength.
The Lord delights in those who revere him,
in those who wait for his love.

15

Exile

She joined our firm as a personnel officer. I did not notice when she arrived, but I quickly became aware of her presence. She was small, dark-haired, vivacious, very smart and attractive, and genuinely interested in each one of us. We naturally responded. It seemed that we had known her for years when we were saddened to learn that she was leaving. Much as she, too, enjoyed working with us and living in England, she was to emigrate to America. Her husband was being posted to New York. She told us the news with a smile, for she was going in order to remain with 'the man in my life'. Had she not been able to accompany him, I am sure that she would have tried to conceal her sadness but, for her, everything would have become infected with some pain until she knew a firm reunion date.

The Jewish Levite (formerly an assistant to the priests at the Temple) would have fully understood those reactions. He was in exile near Mount Hermon, over a hundred miles from Jerusalem. He had been used to 'lead the rejoicing crowd into the house of God'. Now, he was suffering not only the physical separation, but also the continual mockery of his enemies. 'Where is your God?' they would taunt him. Inwardly, he felt that God, his rock, had forgotten him.

What is so impressive about this psalmist is that he notes, admits and understands his condition in an unselfpitying way. He keeps asking himself:

Why are you cast down, my soul,
why groan within me?

He knows the answer, and each time he can repeat it triumphantly and joyfully:

Hope in God; I will praise him still,
my saviour and my God.

Because he has such a firm underlying faith and trust, he can ease himself by pouring out his soul, and he does that in beautiful poetry. Psalm 41 begins:

Like the deer that yearns
for running streams,
so my soul is yearning
for you, my God.

The image of the deer suggests a sentence from the Song of Songs spoken by the bride: 'My Beloved is like a gazelle, like a young stag' (2:9). Further, the yearning, deeply loving words have movingly inspired the composers Palestrina ('Sicut cervus') and, more recently, Howells ('Like as the hart'), and also the artist Eric Gill.

Using a phrase resembling that of the modern personnel officer, the psalmist continues:

My soul is thirsting for God,
the God of my life;
when can I enter and see
the face of God?

God is central for him, and he longs to be in the Temple, in God's presence. Yet despite all his sadness, for:

My tears have become my bread,
by night, by day,

he never falls into the trap of trying to bargain with God.

Bring my soul out of this prison
and then I shall praise your name

was a prayer made in Psalm 141. The Levite manages to praise God unconditionally and call him saviour in the midst of his sufferings, even in God's seeming abandonment of him.

The psalm contains references to running streams, tears and thirst. Suddenly, the chaotic power of water is let loose:

> Deep is calling on deep,
> in the roar of waters;
> your torrents and all your waves
> swept over me.

What is the Levite's response? Somehow, he remains calm:

> By day the Lord will send
> his loving kindness;
> by night I will sing to him,
> praise the God of my life.

The poem continues as Psalm 42:

> Defend me, O God, and plead my cause
> against a godless nation.
> From deceitful and cunning men
> rescue me, O God.

> Since you, O God, are my stronghold,
> why have you rejected me?
> Why do I go mourning
> oppressed by the foe?

> O send forth your light and your truth;
> let these be my guide.
> Let them bring me to your holy mountain
> to the place where you dwell.

And I will come to the altar of God,
the God of my joy.
My redeemer, I will thank you on the harp,
O God, my God.

Why are you cast down, my soul,
why groan within me?
Hope in God; I will praise him still,
my saviour and my God.

The Levite cannot escape from reality. Like us, he remains an exile. In contrast to him, though, we have the great comfort and assistance of knowing when we call God our saviour, that Christ has lived, suffered, died and risen again for us.

16

Exile – The return

Were you brought up to ignore dreams? Did you ever learn the words from the old 'Penny Catechism': 'The first Commandment forbids... superstitious practices, such as... trusting to... dreams, and such like fooleries'? Those are strong words; but when something very like a dream happens in real life, how are we to react?

Such an experience was mine, after I came through a long period of desolation, accompanied latterly by a gradual turning to God in a new way. Suddenly, however, events moved fast. Action taken against me completely stunned me mentally. I continued to live during that weekend, but it was as though my mind and body had separated. I seemed to be watching what I was doing and how I was behaving as an outsider, amazed that there was no emotion left in me. A comparison to a lying in a tomb would not be inappropriate. Then the solution came. When it was offered to me, I recognised that this was the answer. Further, a new way of life would open up for me.

Gradually, this life fell into place, but I had been fundamentally changed. In contrast to before, I was relaxed, because I had known as never before that God is always my constant and true support. The relaxation showed in my features and in an unconscious readiness to smile. I experienced joy. I started to revel in singing again, as I used to do at school. My largely unused voice had not gone. Others, including those who had caused my great problem, noticed and commented on my change, which continued in an obvious way for several months.

That was a personal liberation and a kind of resurrection. Former prisoners and many other people have experienced various forms of the recovery of freedom, from physical as well as from mental deprivation. The people of Israel suffered very harshly, too, as exiles in Babylon. Psalm 136 contains a flash-back account of how, by the rivers, they 'sat and wept, remembering Sion' and hung up their harps on the poplars there, incapable of giving their oppressors the joy of hearing a song. As their desolation had been great, so was their return home wonderful. Psalm 125 gives some indications of that:

> When the Lord delivered Sion from bondage,
> it seemed like a dream.
> Then was our mouth filled with laughter,
> on our lips there were songs.

> The heathens themselves said: 'What marvels
> the Lord worked for them!'
> What marvels the Lord worked for us!
> Indeed we were glad.

> Deliver us, O Lord, from our bondage
> as streams in dry land.
> Those who are sowing in tears
> will sing when they reap.

> They go out, they go out, full of tears,
> carrying seed for the sowing:
> they come back, they come back, full of song,
> carrying their sheaves.

It seems that the Israelites did not fully grasp what had happened to them until the heathens were struck and commented. That was like a confirmatory revelation. Even in the fuller gladness that followed, though, they acknowledged that there remained a need of delivery from a residual bondage. They had not yet entered the kingdom of God.

The final verse of Psalm 125 is full of meaning. When we are called on to suffer, or are merely low and dispirited, we still have with us the seed of God's Word. That seed might seem insignificant, and its presence have to be evidenced only in small, unnoticed ways. If, nevertheless, it is sown, the seed is capable of growth and increase. A great harvest can eventually come from little things.

17

Harvest

Students of English literature are taught about the importance of T.S. Eliot's use of the 'chorus' in his play on Thomas à Becket, *Murder in the Cathedral*. The poor women of Canterbury modelled on the chorus of an ancient Greek drama, watch, and have some part in, the main action. The idea can be extended to apply to the liturgy. The sanctuary can be compared to a stage and all that takes place on it to a play, with the celebrant and the servers representing the principal actors. The congregation may then be regarded as members of a chorus.

Some psalms strongly suggest that the refrains included were intended to be sung or chanted by the Jewish congregations centuries before Christ. Reforms in the Catholic Church's liturgy following Vatican II, designed to encourage the people's participation, may not be so innovative after all. In Psalm 79, a refrain of one verse comes twice near the beginning, and recurs again at the very end:

God of hosts, bring us back;
let your face shine on us and we shall be saved.

Psalm 66 is shorter with the refrain coming regularly throughout:

Let the peoples praise you, O God;
let all the peoples praise you.

The contrast in mood is obvious. Further, what is striking about the second example is the generosity of the expressed desire that the God of Israel should be praised by the whole of humanity. The argument to reach that is somewhat complicated. God is asked to continue blessing the Jews, partly by granting material prosperity. If he saves them, then the other nations will notice and will come to learn his ways of justice and fairness. In any event, he is not distanced from them: he already rules them. Consequently, it is to be hoped that they will all praise him.

The first verse recalls the wording of God's blessing for Aaron to give to the sons of Israel (Num 6:24-26):

May the Lord bless you and keep you.
May the Lord let his face shine on you and be gracious to you.
May the Lord uncover his face to you and bring you peace.

The peaceful and pastoral ending of the psalm suggests a harvest song.

O God, be gracious and bless us
and let your face shed its light upon us.
So will your ways be known upon earth
and all nations learn your saving help.

Let the peoples praise you, O God;
Let all the peoples praise you.

Let the nations be glad and exult
for you rule the world with justice.
With fairness you rule the peoples,
you guide the nations on earth.

Let the peoples praise you, O God;
let all the peoples praise you.

The earth has yielded its fruit
for God, our God, has blessed us.
May God still give us his blessing
till the ends of the earth revere him.

Let the peoples praise you, O God;
let all the peoples praise you.

The liberality in approach of this psalm is reflected in
the prayer of Jesus at the Last Supper, 'May they all be
one' (Jn 17:21-23), and in the underlying longings of the
twentieth century ecumenical movement.

18

Pilgrimage (1)

It is well known in this country that birds can be adaptable.
Blue tits somehow learned that, if they pierced the shining
tops on milk bottles, there would be cream below which
they would like to drink. Robins can nest in unexpected
places, such as in a disused watering can. These birds
naturally keep a part of their fear of a possible attacker, but
they trust us to respect them. In return, they can delight us
by laying their eggs and raising their brood in a relatively
unprotected spot.

Occasionally, pigeons or sparrows fly into a church's
open door; but they soon become frightened, unable to find
the way out, and flutter around avoiding human attempts to
help them. It is probably unusual over here for a bird to
build a nest in a church. That, however, provided a delicate
image for the writer of Psalm 83. He was on his way to
Jerusalem and was already captivated by the thought of
seeing the Temple's beauty:

> How lovely is your dwelling place,
> Lord, God of hosts.

His soul was longing and yearning for it, because it was
God's house; but deep within him he was really trying to
express his love for God:

> My heart and my soul ring out their joy
> to God, the living God.

> The sparrow herself finds a home
> and the swallow a nest for her brood;

she lays her young by your altars,
Lord of hosts, my king and my God.

He had a certain reverence for the birds. They could fly
easily to the Temple and live there; but he had to continue
journeying to reach it. He idealised those who could be in it
often, and who were continually singing God's praises.

The idea of being a pilgrim is developed. Travellers
who have in their hearts the roads to Sion are happy:

As they go through the Bitter Valley
they make it a place of springs,
the autumn rain covers it with blessings.
They walk with ever growing strength,
they will see the God of gods in Sion.

These pilgrims become closer to God and stronger in
their journeying, for they go in sure hope. They even give
his blessings to their own dry, dull surroundings. They
will soon reach their final destination, and enter God's
presence.

The tone of the psalm changes to a petition to God for
the king. Again, the desirability of the Temple is stressed: a
day there is better than a thousand elsewhere. The conclusion is triumphant:

For the Lord God is a rampart, a shield;
he will give us his favour and glory.
The Lord will not refuse any good
to those who walk without blame.

Lord, God of hosts,
happy the man who trusts in you!

Pilgrimage (2)

In the English countryside, there are two habitats for our national tree, the oak: open meadows and woodlands. I can visualise one oak growing alone in the middle of a large field in Surrey. It is quite old, spreads widely, is not very tall, looks beautiful, but gives the impression of crouching on the ground. In contrast, the sight of oaks in woodlands can, I find, give me thoughts of a silent though vital struggle. There is not sufficient room for the small trees to branch out sideways, while more mature, larger trees block much of the light from above. The small oaks do not passively accept a harsh confinement. They respond by shooting up towards the sky. In so doing, they produce much valuable straight timber.

When reading the start of Psalm 120, I often think of the resourceful woodland oaks. Life can, at times, seem to hem us in tightly on all sides; but are the circumstances ones which we should accept, or ones which we should seek to change to some degree or even reject? These questions can also arise frequently as we try to follow, in its details, God's plan for each of us.

The psalm itself contains an image of a traveller who is in a valley surrounded by lofty mountains. He has little choice but to look upwards for help. He asks from where exactly that help will come. The atmosphere is quiet. There is no suggestion that foes are on the high slopes watching every movement of the unprotected psalmist and ready to attack him at any moment they choose. Alternatively, when he looks up, he may see sacred places of false gods on the heights. His words could then mean that at once he discards any notion of assistance from them.

The phrasing of the answer to the question raised may

be familiar to you. The verse is used in the solemn form of blessing by a bishop:

My help shall come from the Lord
who made heaven and earth.

The Latin, too, is fairly well known:

Adiutorium nostrum in nomine Domini
qui fecit caelum et terram.

Is not it an almost overwhelming thought that the Almighty Creator of light, and of heaven, earth and the seas with everything in them (the story is picturesquely told in the first chapter of Genesis) provides us with help? We do not easily accept that he has unconditional love for us. His complete trustworthiness and availability may also be difficult for us to grasp, for most people find it extremely hard to retain fully their own initial honesty and integrity. Frequently, of course, God uses other human beings as his instruments to help us. In particular, Christ, who is God made man, helps and saves us.

The remainder of the psalm seems to be spoken to him by a companion of the psalmist. It explains that we may inadvertently stumble on our journey or need to sleep, or we may find conditions onerous or even malevolent. Nevertheless, the Lord remains our guard and guide whenever and wherever we need him. We merely have to call on him for help.

The psalm is used in Evening Prayer on some Fridays and in the Office for the Dead. That adds a poignancy to the final verse. When we go from this life to eternity, the Lord himself will continue to guard us.

I lift up my eyes to the mountains:
from where shall come my help?
My help shall come from the Lord
who made heaven and earth.

May he never allow you to stumble!
Let him sleep not, your guard.
No, he sleeps not nor slumbers,
Israel's guard.

The Lord is your guard and your shade;
at your right side he stands.
By day the sun shall not smite you
nor the moon in the night.

The Lord will guard you from evil,
he will guard your soul.
The Lord will guard your going and coming
both now and for ever.

20

Jerusalem

The holiday had been advertised as a tour of the Yorkshire and Derbyshire dales. I had not seen those lovely parts of England before, and I particularly noticed that the itinerary included Rievaulx, about 25 miles South-West of Whitby and famous for the ruins of its mediaeval Cistercian abbey. In the sixth form at school, I had studied monasticism in England in the twelfth century, and Aelred of Rievaulx seemed like a friend. Imagine my feelings of expectation, then, when the coach was travelling along the road leading towards the place. However, this was not a pilgrimage and the other members of the party had varying interests, so that, on reaching the site, the courier asked whether anyone would like to get out. At once, I loudly and yearningly replied, 'Yes', and fortunately several other travellers agreed. Those impressive ruins were well worth our visit. They still held a religious presence.

No doubt you can recall having similar feelings of excitement when approaching some place which is very special to you. Such reactions are human and timeless. Our anticipation helps to make the place seem great and beautiful. These thoughts came very strongly to Jews when on pilgrimage to Jerusalem, the city of God, which had unique associations for them as a people. It represented the earthly centre of their lives and hopes. The Temple for divine worship was there, and Solomon had built a Hall of Justice. The name, Jerusalem, was interpreted to mean peace (*shalom* in Hebrew).

Psalm 121 is one of a series of 'songs of ascents', probably meaning that it was sung by pilgrims on the hilly way up to Jerusalem for one the feasts. Its heartfelt joy still touches us today. The psalmist first talks of his delight at the initial news of the forthcoming journey, hard though the actual circumstances of it may have been, Then he moves mentally immediately to the present, addressing Jerusalem with great affection. He is there! He admires the compactness of the city and its special purposes. He makes a touching, widely embracing prayer for peace, in palaces and homes, between families and friends.

I rejoiced when I heard them say:
'Let us go to God's house.'
And now our feet are standing
within your gates, O Jerusalem.

Jerusalem is built as a city
strongly compact.
It is there that the tribes go up,
the tribes of the Lord.

For Israel's law it is,
there to praise the Lord's name.
There were set the thrones of judgment
of the house of David.

For the peace of Jerusalem pray:
'Peace be to your homes!
May peace reign in your walls,
in your palaces, peace!'

For love of my brethren and friends
I say: 'Peace upon you!'
For love of the house of the Lord
I will ask for your good.

21

Law, divine

What proportion of the pedestrians going along much used London thoroughfares notice the pieces of grass often growing at the edges of some of the paving stones? Those blades are like a challenge by life to a rigid, contrived and manufactured order.

Some systems are, of course, necessary if civilisation as we know it is to survive, and that applies also to languages. It is interesting that thousands of years ago, the Jews were exploiting possible shapes for their language, Hebrew. The psalms were composed in poetic form, which gave them beauty, helped in the memorising of them and provided rhythms for chants.

Occasionally, a psalmist went further, and introduced complexity in layout, for the pleasure of using his brain to the glory of God. Psalms 110 and 111, for example, have half-lines starting with successive letters of the Hebrew alphabet. Such poems are called acrostics, an early kind of word game. In Psalm 144 each of the 22 Hebrew letters has one full verse to itself, while in Psalm 36 the number of verses per letter is two.

The masterpiece of these designs is Psalm 118. It is the longest in the Psalter, with 176 verses. The first Hebrew letter begins each of the first 8 verses; the second Hebrew letter begins each verse of the second group of 8 verses; and so on for the other 20 letters in turn. Not only this, but the psalmist, who wrote in praise of the divine revealed Law or Torah, used the word 'law' or a word of similar meaning (such as will, ways, word, precepts, rulings, commands, decrees, statutes) in nearly every verse. Sometimes he managed to include two such words in the verse.

It is probable that the psalmist was an intelligent young

lawyer. His dedication to and enthusiasm for the divine Law and for his writing were not suppressed by his heavy, self-imposed system. Admittedly the psalm is not as appealing as are many of the others, and by keeping to his arrangement the psalmist could not readily allow his thoughts to progress. What is delightful, though, is to find a poetical blade of grass or flower appearing from under the concrete form. That shows joy in the performance of God's Will of Love.

Here is a specimen, part XIV (vv. 105-112) of the psalm. Incidentally, the first two lines of it illustrate the use of parallelism, which means that one idea is expressed in two similar ways.

> Your word is a lamp for my steps
> and a light for my path.
> I have sworn and have made up my mind
> to obey your decrees.
>
> Lord, I am deeply afflicted:
> by your word give me life.
> Accept, Lord, the homage of my lips
> and teach me your decrees.
>
> Though I carry my life in my hands,
> I remember your law.
> Though the wicked try to ensnare me
> I do not stray from your precepts.
>
> Your will is my heritage for ever,
> the joy of my heart.
> I set myself to carry out your will
> in fulness, for ever.

In that translation, two lines represent one verse. Naturally enough, no attempt was made to start each of the 8 verses with the same letter.

It may seem that the psalmist must have been insincere,

pedantic and self-opinionated. Why did not he let himself write simply? Why be so artificial? Big does not necessarily mean beautiful, and within his own limitations he could not avoid repetition.

Nevertheless, the whole psalm reveals a deep longing to praise God and to thank him for the wonders of his merciful dealings with humanity. It emphasises the importance of behaving as he wishes if we are to come to him and so be happy. There is no need to read all 176 verses at the same time, and in the Church's Office normally only one group of 8 verses is recited on any one occasion. Then, the poetical, personal touches can be better appreciated. Among those, the final verses, 175-176, are noteworthy:

Give life to my soul that I may praise you.
Let your decrees give me help.
I am lost like a sheep; seek your servant
for I remember your commands.

22

Christ as Messiah

When Moses, made curious by observing a bush blazing with fire but not being burnt up, went closer to it, God called out to him: 'Come no nearer. Take off your shoes, for the place on which you stand is holy ground' (Ex 3:2-5).

That might sum up my feelings about Psalm 109. The text and meaning of the psalm are also uncertain, but the Church uses it very frequently: on many solemnities and major feasts, and on nearly every Sunday of the year. It relates to the Messiah, and Jesus quoted its first verse to the Pharisees, baffling them with his questioning:

> The Lord's revelation to my Master:
> 'Sit on my right:
> your foes I will put beneath your feet.'

They thought that the Christ would be David's son, but were unable to explain how David as the inspired psalmist could call him Lord. Matthew commented that afterwards no one dared to question Jesus further (22:41-46), while at the end of his similar account Mark declared that 'the great majority of the people heard this with delight' (12:37). Peter was clearly impressed too; near the conclusion of his first address to the people at Pentecost, he repeated the quotation, emphasising that 'David himself never went up to heaven', and he finally declared that Israel could be certain that Jesus was both Lord and Christ (Acts 2:34-36). Further, Paul in his First Letter to the Corinthians considered how the last line of verse 1 meant that Christ must be king until all his enemies (including death) had been subjected to him. Then he as Son would be subject to the Father 'so that God may be all in all' (15:25-28).

The psalm continues:

The Lord will wield from Sion
your sceptre of power:
rule in the midst of all your foes.

A prince from the day of your birth
on the holy mountains;
from the womb before the dawn I begot you.

The Lord has sworn an oath he will not change.
'You are a priest for ever,
a priest like Melchizedek of old.'

The Master standing at your right hand
will shatter kings in the day of his wrath.

He shall drink from the stream by the wayside
and therefore he shall lift up his head.

Chapter 7 of the Letter to the Hebrews contains an analysis of Christ's priesthood by reference to the fourth verse of this psalm. The Letter speaks of the perpetual existence of Melchizedek and how the great patriarch Abraham paid him tithes in acknowledgement of his superiority. The psalm, it declares, referred to a new priesthood, of the same order as Melchizedek (not as Aaron). Jesus did not belong to Aaron's tribe, and in him the earlier law was abolished. He cannot lose his priesthood, because he remains for ever. He is perfect, and his power to save is utterly certain.

23

Christ – Good Friday (1)

As a Jewish boy, Jesus studied the Scriptures, and nearly two thousand years later we can experience a sense of immediacy and even direct contact with him when we read a psalm from which he quoted. A famous example of such use by him was at the time of the crucifixion. Mark reported (15:33-37) that there had been darkness over the whole land for about three hours. Jesus then cried out in a loud voice: 'Eloi, Eloi, lama sabachthani?' which means: 'My God, my God, why have you forsaken me?' Soon afterwards, he 'gave a loud cry and breathed his last.'

Jesus had cried out the beginning of Psalm 21. Despite his growing weakness and his racking pains, he may have been able to think a little about the words of that familiar psalm at some time during the three-hour period before his death. The gospel accounts of Mark and of Matthew give him little chance (or strength) to have done that after his final loud cry. How might the psalm have helped him?

It does not say what had caused the intense suffering of the psalmist, but he is near to death. His initial, heartfelt plea is to God who seems to have forsaken him. He has called by day and by night without receiving any reply or the gift of peace. However, he still acknowledges that God is his God. He declares that God is holy and recalls that, when his forefathers trusted in him, it was never in vain.

His present plight, though, is terrible. He is 'a worm and no man, scorned by men, despised by the people.' Everyone mocks him, especially for his continued trust in the Lord. Surely, they were no doubt thinking, he must be a great sinner if he has to suffer like that. His prayer again changes to dwell on trust in God, who has protected him from the moment of his birth. From then, too, God has remained his God.

> Do not leave me alone in my distress;
> come close, there is none else to help.

The psalm can give us assistance in how to pray when we ourselves are in great difficulties. We may not feel his presence, but God will come closer to us if we can pray like that. We are not to try to tell him how or when to save us, but he will surely do so in his own wonderful manner if we commit ourselves wholly to his care.

The psalmist returns to his own present situation. Ferocious wild animals, bulls and lions, seem to surround him. Physically he is poured out and his bones seem disjointed. His throat is parched like clay, and his tongue sticks to his mouth. That sounds like a description of a fever, but he continues:

> (The wicked) tear holes in my hands and my feet
> and lay me in the dust of death.
>
> I can count every one of my bones.
> These people stare at me and gloat;
> they divide my clothing among them.
> They cast lots for my robe.

Despite the seeming imminence of death, he summons up strength to make yet another moving petition to God:

> O Lord, do not leave me alone,
> my strength, make haste to help me!

He vividly implores God that his soul should be rescued and his life saved from sword, dogs, lions and oxen. Then, an amazing change in mood occurs. Without any explanations, he suddenly appears to be calm and well, and he promises:

I will tell of your name to my brethren
and praise you where they are assembled.

A moment ago, he was on the point of death. How did
God save him?

The remaining verses, composed presumably by the
same psalmist later on, are filled with praise and thanksgiving to God and exhortations to all Israelites to revere him,
for 'he heard the poor man when he cried.' There is some
prophetic writing, that all shall return to the Lord and
worship him:

And my soul shall live for him, my children serve him.
They shall tell of the Lord to generations yet to come,
declare his faithfulness to peoples yet unborn:
'These things the Lord has done.'

24

Christ – Good Friday (2)

Just before Jesus breathed his last on the cross, he said: 'Father, into your hands I commend my spirit' (Lk 23:46). He was praying words from the fifth verse of Psalm 30. That verse continues: 'It is you who will redeem me, Lord.' His death in such terrible circumstances was to give a new meaning to redemption, and so to our understanding of suffering.

The psalm begins:

In you, O Lord, I take refuge.
Let me never be put to shame.

There is an appeal to be set free and for the rescue to come speedily, but from what is not clear. God is called a rock and a stronghold, and he is asked, for his own sake, to lead the psalmist. Their wills are virtually at one, for the psalmist commits himself to God. So the psalmist has the courage to plead in effect that, should God abandon him, not only would he himself be humbled, but respect for God would also be lessened, for many people would have known of the psalmist's unconditional trust in him. No matter what physical or emotional suffering might assail the psalmist, he tries to remain spiritually fixed on God. Since the Lord detests those who worship false gods, the psalmist can confidently request gladness and joy in his love.

Still directly addressing God, this portion of the psalm ends:

You who have seen my affliction
and taken heed of my soul's distress,
have not handed me over to the enemy,
but set my feet at large.

As though another psalm begins here, the tone changes rather abruptly, and a further complaint is made. This time, the psalmist is in deep distress, with sorrow, sighs and affliction. Even his bones waste away. The trouble is not entirely physical. His foes reproach him; his neighbours scorn him; and his friends fear him. Strangers in the street run away at his approach. He is forgotten, like a dead man or something thrown away.

He has heard slander spoken against him. He is in constant fear while plots are made to take his life. Again, however, he manages to make a beautiful act of trust:

> But as for me, I trust in you, Lord,
> I say: 'You are my God.
> My life is in your hands, deliver me
> from the hands of those who hate me.
>
> Let your face shine on your servant.
> Save me in your love.'

The third portion of this psalm is concerned with praise and thanksgiving. It commences:

> How great is the goodness, Lord,
> that you keep for those who fear you,
> that you show to those who trust you
> in the sight of men.

God has vindicated his servant, and he hides and shelters all his faithful. In a short play-back of the time of affliction, the psalmist admits:

> 'I am far removed from your sight'
> I said in my alarm.
> Yet you heard the voice of my plea
> when I cried for help.

That verse may be applied to Christ who had on the cross cried out to God asking why he had forsaken him, but who, on the third day, was to rise triumphant over death. Next, it is asserted that God avenges those who behave proudly, and a final call is made to all who hope in him to be strong and to take courage. The psalmist has lived out what he now testifies.

25

Christ – Holy Saturday (1)

St John may have written his Letters as an old man. If so, by then he would have thought much and deeply about the mysteries of Jesus and his life and of the Christian way of life. He was able to stand back from the facts and to summarise his conclusions, hardly elaborating on how he had reached them: God is love, and we are to live as his children, loving him and one another.

When reading Psalm 15, I cannot decide whether its author of earlier days resembled an elderly St John, or whether he was a young, inexperienced man, perhaps a priest. I have the impression that he may still have to learn some of life's lessons, or that he may even have been a late convert to God's service.

The psalm begins:

Preserve me, God, I take refuge in you.
I say to the Lord: 'You are my God.
My happiness lies in you alone.'

This can be read like a petition for the future by some-one who has recently turned to God, and has not yet been shown to be faithful in the face of severe trials. There is no mention of thanks or praise. The words seem to be rather self-orientated. Then he considers his 'marvellous love for the faithful ones' of God's land. He claims association with them, and declares confidently that he will never worship false gods, for 'Those who choose other gods increase their sorrows.' Jesus considered that, but from the opposite an-gle, when he said: 'Come to me, all you who labour and are overburdened, and I will give you rest... Yes, my yoke is easy and my burden light' (Mt 11:28,30).

The psalmist then rejoices at his lot in life, with God as his prize, and his heritage as welcome. He blesses the Lord who advises him and 'even at night directs (his) heart'. Has he never felt the darkness and fear of night, or been plagued by mental anguish? He carries on strongly that he keeps God in his sight, for 'since he is at my right hand, I shall stand firm.' Has he, I wonder, ever experienced a withdrawal of the awareness of God's presence? Is he now being overconfident and lacking in humility?

Whether the psalmist has recently let himself be found by God, or has gone through many trials and become close to him, he now uses words which could have been adopted by Christ himself. Peter, in fact, quoted them with the previous verse in his first address to the crowds at Pentecost (Acts 2:25-28):

And so my heart rejoices, my soul is glad;
even my body shall rest in safety.
For you will not leave my soul among the dead,
nor let your beloved know decay.

You will show me the path of life,
the fulness of joy in your presence,
at your right hand happiness for ever.

How do you react to this psalm? Could it be entirely prophetic, about Christ? Then, the queries and qualifications could be ignored.

26

Christ – Holy Saturday (2)

At one time, Holy Saturday always seemed to me to be empty and dead. The Church's ceremonies on Maundy Thursday and Good Friday had been magnificent, stimulating and very prayerful. Then, there would be nothing until the Easter Vigil. The gap was almost tangible. I did not understand its meaning until I experienced a profound trial which continued over quite a long period. Afterwards I had a few days' break. That rest relaxed me and prepared me for a complete, lovely, unexpected change in circumstances. The break has been vitally important; without it I would have been exhausted and could hardly have realised the full implications of the change.

So, but in a far more wonderful manner, is it with Holy Saturday. That is a day of preparation and anticipation for the victory of Easter. Jesus' time in the tomb was a proof that he had really died. His resurrection was initially a matter for incredulity on the part of many of his followers, until they believed and were filled with joy.

Holy Saturday may be described as a paradoxical day. It is not what it appears to be. Those who put Christ to death were not the victors. He would soon re-appear in a glorified body. Those who grieved for him would rejoice as never before. The first psalm used at Morning Prayer, Psalm 63, foreshadows these circumstances, although it is primarily concerned with the punishment of slanderers and the saving of the just man. The wicked 'aim bitter words like arrows', but God has his own single arrow with which he shoots them. Divine retribution follows their conspiracies; God intervenes in a mysterious way. That causes all to fear, while his people give him glory.

Hear my voice, O God, as I complain,
guard my life from dread of the foe.
Hide me from the band of the wicked,
from the throng of those who do evil.

They sharpen their tongues like swords;
they aim bitter words like arrows
to shoot at the innocent from ambush,
shooting suddenly and recklessly.

They scheme their evil course;
they conspire to lay secret snares.
They say: 'Who will see us?
Who can search out our crimes?'

He will search who searches the mind
and knows the depths of the heart.
God has shot them with his arrow
and dealt them sudden wounds.
Their own tongue has brought them to ruin
and all who see them mock.

Then will all men fear;
they will tell what God has done.
They will understand God's deeds.
The just will rejoice in the Lord
and fly to him for refuge.
All the upright hearts will glory.

27

Christ – Easter Sunday

Early on that morning in August 1972, the telephone had rung unexpectedly. The nurse gave my family the news that our father had died. He had had only a short illness. As we were ready first, I drove my priest-brother to the hospital. Going along an easy, straight piece of road, some Latin words came from nowhere into my mind. I would now say that they were put there by the action of the Holy Spirit: 'Haec dies quam fecit Dominus: exsultemus, et laetemur in ea' ('This day was made by the Lord; we rejoice and are glad'). The car was approaching traffic-lights, and I did not then wonder what was the source of that Latin. Much later, its significance forcibly struck me. The words are a verse from Psalm 117 and were used in the Gradual for Easter Sunday Mass in the Tridentine Rite. The Gradual was sung before the hymn *Victimae paschali*, and both were very memorable.

The psalm was a processional hymn for use on the feast of Tabernacles when the Jews celebrated their delivery from slavery in Egypt. We would regard it as a hymn of rejoicing in salvation. It starts with a general invitation to thank God:

Give thanks to the Lord for he is good,
for his love endures for ever.

Then groups consisting of the sons of Israel, the sons of Aaron and the fearers of the Lord (or the faithful) are each invited to say: 'His love endures for ever.' That refrain is used to make a litany in another psalm (Ps 135) where it comes alternately with a line of the text recalling God's marvellous works and his saving action.

In Psalm 117, a different single voice, possibly that of the king, seems to come in, reporting how he called to the Lord who answered and freed him. With the Lord beside him, he does not fear. Men cannot do anything against him. He emphasises, twice, that:

It is better to take refuge in the Lord
than to trust in men (or, in princes).

Using repetition again, he expansively tells how 'the nations all encompassed' him like bees, but in the Lord's name he crushed them.

Now there is rejoicing on account of God's intervention:

I was hard-pressed and was falling
but the Lord came to help me.
The Lord is my strength and my song;
he is my saviour...

The Lord's right hand has triumphed;
his right hand raised me.
The Lord's right hand has triumphed;
I shall not die, I shall live
and recount his deeds.
I was punished, I was punished by the Lord,
but not doomed to die.

Those verses direct our thoughts as Christians to Jesus' triumph over death. Soon after, come two verses which were quoted by him in the Temple when, early in the first Holy Week, he told the parable of the wicked husbandmen:

The stone which the builders rejected
has become the corner stone.
This is the work of the Lord,
a marvel in our eyes.

Jesus commented that the kingdom of God would be taken from the chief priests and scribes and given to a people who would produce its fruit (Mt 21:42-43). Peter, too, as a prisoner, used the first verse in addressing the rulers and elders about the healing of a cripple through the power of the risen Christ (Acts 4:11).

Next in the psalm come the verse witnessing that the day was made by the Lord and a petition from several people directly to God to grant salvation and success. When the crowds shouted at Jesus on Palm Sunday, they used part of the following verse (Mt 21:9):

Blessed in the name of the Lord
is he who comes.

Another voice speaks, directing the people about the feast's processional liturgy (Lev 23:40):

Go forward in procession with branches
even to the altar.

Touchingly, the psalm continues:

You are my God, I thank you.
My God, I praise you.

It concludes as it began:

Give thanks to the Lord for he is good;
for his love endures for ever.

28

Sin

Many Christians probably find it difficult and testing to relate charitably to those who are behaving sinfully. However, we too are sinners and are affected by sin; it can also be painful to discover the extent of our sinfulness. There were no such qualms for the writer of Psalm 35. He saw humanity as composed of two rather impossibly tidy groups: the just and the sinners. Still, some of his insights may be helpful to us.

The psalm begins with a caricature of the sinner. The first verse is a horrible summary:

> Sin speaks to the sinner
> in the depths of his heart.
> There is no fear of God
> before his eyes.

Without respect for God, we can hardly progress, and it is possible for us to drive him out from our innermost being. The psalm speaks of moral distortions of bodily parts and senses – deceit in the sinner's mouth, evil ways for his feet, a general clinging to evil. Worse, he is ignorant of his condition:

> He so flatters himself in his mind
> that he knows not his guilt...
> All wisdom is gone.

The death-like mood suddenly changes to a vibrant, liberating one of light, life and love. Addressing the Lord from now on, the psalmist declares that God's love and truth reach to heaven; and that, while his justice resembles

the highest sacred mountain, his judgments are correspond-
ingly deep. He protects man and beast alike.

O Lord, how precious is your love.

The psalmist has looked at the horror and crookedness
of sin with revulsion. He comments that men 'find refuge
in the shelter of your wings'. That recalls for us Jesus'
sad words of rebuke for the holy city: 'Jerusalem, Jerusalem, you that kill the prophets and stone those who are
sent to you! How often have I longed to gather your children, as a hen gathers her chicks under her wings, and
you refused! So be it!' (Mt 23:37).

Instead of being shut in on self, the psalm continues
that the faithful feast and drink on God's riches and
delight. That is the true end which he made for each of
us:

In you is the source of life
and in your light we see light.

Without God, we can do and be nothing. St Paul would
tell the Ephesians (5:8,10-11): 'You were darkness once,
but now you are light in the Lord... Try to discover what
the Lord wants of you, having nothing to do with the futile
works of darkness but exposing them by contrast.'

There follows a tactful request to God, that he would
reward those who are faithful to him:

Keep on loving those who know you,
doing justice for upright hearts.

The problem that the wicked often prosper in this world
is not directly faced. A flicker of fear then intrudes, since
the psalmist is under no illusions about the unpleasantness
of coming into contact with sinners. He begs that the proud
man may not crush him nor the wicked expel him. Finally,
he allows himself to gloat in anticipation of the fall of evil-

doers, who 'shall never arise'. Perhaps that refers to hell in the next life. Christ, though, was to reveal to us the extent and depth of the love of God, who tries to reclaim to himself in this life even the most hardened sinners.

29

Pride

The ancient Greeks, so the saying goes, had a word for it. The Greek word in my mind is *hubris* which, according to the *Oxford English Dictionary*, means 'insolent pride or security'. Tragedies have been written about the capacity of some human beings to overreach themselves. They stretch out, figuratively, further than is appropriate, for they have not accepted their innate limitations. In effect, they try to behave like gods.

The writer of Psalm 29 candidly admits that he went too far:

> I said to myself in my good fortune:
> 'Nothing will ever disturb me.'
> Your favour had set me on a mountain fastness,
> then you hid your face and I was put to confusion.

His arrogance made him view life falsely, and he neglected to thank God for giving him his existence and all the many benefits which he enjoyed in life. He took everything for granted. He imagined that his material well-being would be immortal. He felt unassailable because the wheel of fortune favoured him, and he may have segregated himself from others.

God, in his loving providence, wanted him to see his errors and repent. Just as can happen to any of us, the psalmist's circumstances changed. He was ill-prepared for that. However, God was merciful, and did not say to him the words used by Christ in his parable about hoarding possessions: 'Fool! This very night the demand will be made for your soul; and this hoard of yours, whose will it be then?' (Lk 12:20). The psalmist, instead, cried and pleaded to God. The argument he employed showed how he had retained some trust in God's mercy:

> What profit would my death be, my going to the grave?
> Can dust give you praise or proclaim your truth?

His belief in an afterlife was rather vague.

God, the loving Father, saw that the sinner had repented. The descriptive words given in the psalm could be helpful for us too: the Lord listened and had pity; he came to help, and he restored to life and healed; his anger lasts a moment but his favour throughout life. In a preview of the parable of the prodigal son, the psalmist declares:

> For me you have changed my mourning into dancing,
> you removed my sackcloth and clothed me with joy.

A lovely aspect of this psalm is that all the verses referred to above follow an introductory verse in praise of God:

> I will praise you, Lord, you have rescued me
> and have not let my enemies rejoice over me.

Further, at the end there is thanksgiving:

> So my soul sings psalms to you unceasingly.
> O Lord my God, I will thank you for ever.

30

Repentance (1)

'Eat less of what you like, and more what you dislike.' Suggestions like that were made to me as a child for what to do during Lent. This one overlooked that enjoying one's food can be beneficial, and also helped to make Lent seem to be a rather negative time in the Church's year. Unfortunately, such an attitude when impressed on a young mind can cling. So my recent experience when saying Morning Prayer on Ash Wednesday could still come as a relief.

The first psalm was Psalm 107, which begins:

My heart is ready, O God;
I will sing, sing your praise.

To have an early, arousing thought about praising God was encouraging. Later, the initial intercession spoke of thanks and love:

As we begin the season of Lent, we give thanks to God the Father for this time of grace. Let us ask him to cleanse our hearts and strengthen us in love through the Holy Spirit.

Perhaps, I considered, it might be possible to read the *Miserere* (Psalm 50) with more emphasis on praise, thanks and love, although it is one of the penitential psalms. After all, the setting by Allegri as sung, for instance, by the choir of St John's College, Cambridge, is soaring, vibrant and inspiring.

Have mercy on me, God, in your kindness.
In your compassion blot out my offence.

O wash me more and more from my guilt
and cleanse me from my sin.

My offences truly I know them;
my sin is always before me.
Against you, you alone, have I sinned;
what is evil in your sight I have done.

That you may be justified when you give sentence
and be without reproach when you judge,
O see, in guilt I was born,
a sinner was I conceived.

Indeed you love truth in the heart;
then in the secret of my heart teach me wisdom.
O purify me, then I shall be clean;
O wash me, I shall be whiter than snow.

Make me hear rejoicing and gladness,
that the bones you have crushed may revive.
From my sins turn away your face
and blot out all my guilt.

A pure heart create for me, O God,
put a steadfast spirit within me.
Do not cast me away from your presence,
nor deprive me of your holy spirit.

In this first portion, the psalmist is very concerned about his need for cleansing from his sin, which may have been some form of deceit. He indicates stages like those for washing a soiled piece of white cloth: first, soap may be rubbed directly onto the worst stains; then the material would be washed in soapy water, and finally rinsed several times in clear water. So, spiritually, the offence has to be removed and the guilt washed out.

The psalmist's concern resembles an obsession. His slightly unbalanced mind keeps reverting to cleansing. He behaves somewhat similarly to the mad Lady Macbeth of Shakespeare's play; but while she wanted to wash her hands free from blood herself, he continually beseeches God to purify him. It is noteworthy that, in his distress, he usually calls the Supreme Being by the especially revered name of 'God' instead of 'Lord'.

The initial plea for mercy brings recollection of God's kindness. It is a reminder of the past good relationship between them. Although the God of the Old Testament can at times appear rather fearsome, the psalmist knows that he has compassion. We can take that further, and meditate on how Jesus suffered for us and suffers in us and with us, and how as members of his Church we have been sacramentally washed with the blood and water which flowed from his pierced side on Calvary.

An important development is the recognition that the sin was against God alone; so the psalmist cannot wash himself. Then a touching plea is introduced. We could interpret the words as meaning that the psalmist was born inescapably affected by original sin. There is an implication that he has been false at heart; but now he almost boldly asks to be taught wisdom, to help him in discrimination for the future. Again, however, his need for cleansing overwhelms him.

His brain seems to revolve in circles around that. Rather like C.S. Lewis found in his book *A Grief Observed*, though, the circles are not closed, for each one rises above the previous one as part of a spiral. There is some real movement and progression upwards. As sinners too, we can find ourselves involved at any place on the spiral, and identify our prayer with that of the psalmist.

Now he admits some physical pain, which could, he claims, be eased by a return to the joys of life. Possibly following God's promises of renewal, conveyed by the prophets Jeremiah and Ezekiel, he asks for there to be a profound inward change in him, like a re-creation of himself. In desolation again, he pleads not to be separated from God and his life-giving spirit.

Give me again the joy of your help;
with a spirit of fervour sustain me,
that I may teach transgressors your ways
and sinners may return to you.

O rescue me, God, my helper,
and my tongue shall ring out your goodness.
O Lord, open my lips
and my mouth shall declare your praise.

For in sacrifice you take no delight,
burnt offering from me you would refuse,
my sacrifice, a contrite spirit.
A humbled, contrite heart you will not spurn.

In your goodness, show favour to Sion:
rebuild the walls of Jerusalem.
Then you will be pleased with lawful sacrifice,
holocausts offered on your altar.

This second portion shows the extent of the psalmist's progress. Not only is there no reference to washing, but he turns his thoughts away from self. He wants to be, as we would say, an apostle. His witness would be all the more impressive because of what he has come through. He promises, now, to praise God on his recovery. (The following verse can be used at the start of the daily Divine Office.) Next, he is willing to offer his spirit as a sacrifice of thanksgiving. He has seen that outward observances are insufficient. Maybe to provide a counterbalance, the final verses were probably a later addition. Their tone is brisker and less prayerful.

The psalm has an introductory note referring to the visit of the prophet Nathan to King David after he had wrongly taken Bathsheba for his wife. Scholars think that the King may not, however, have composed it, at least not on that occasion.

31

Repentance (2)

During the war, the Nazis pillaged, among other places, the Kunsthistorisches Museum in Vienna. A happy result, however, was that, in about 1950, an exhibition was held in London of the recovered art treasures before their return to Vienna.

I can still clearly recall my first sight of Cellini's famous salt cellar, made in the sixteenth century for the King of France. This was no ordinary cruet stand. Cellini had, as it were, sculpted from gold two human figures, a strong masculine Sea and a graceful female Earth. They sat opposite each other on a black ebony base, and the sculpture was enlivened with enamel. I remember standing still, struck and thrilled by this masterpiece. Then I walked slowly around the show-case. I wanted to see this wonder from every angle and to try to fix its appearance in my memory. I visited that exhibition several times, and I always renewed my acquaintance with the salt cellar.

The Church, too, has great spiritual treasures, and she likes and encourages us to view them in different ways, and to keep returning to them. I realised that more deeply with my growing familiarity with the psalms and with Morning and Evening Prayer.

The psalms are among the Church's special jewels, and she shows them to us in different lights. For example, the *De profundis* (Psalm 129) is said, or chanted, at Evening Prayer (Vespers) on Christmas Day. Does that seem surprising to you? Was your immediate reaction on the lines of 'How can that be? Christmas is a festival of life and joy, but the *De profundis* arouses thoughts of death and sadness.' The Church, it is true, encourages us to pray the *De profundis* for the dead, but with the hope of resurrection. It may also be helpful to bear in mind that, to the actual psalm, we often add a couple of sentences – especially when we are using the older translation:

Eternal rest give unto them, O Lord,
and let perpetual light shine upon them.
May they rest in peace. Amen.

Those words do not form part of the psalm itself. In a fairly recent translation, Psalm 129 alone reads:

Out of the depths I cry to you, O Lord,
Lord, hear my voice!
O let your ears be attentive
to the voice of my pleading.

If you, O Lord, should mark our guilt,
Lord, who would survive?
But with you is found forgiveness:
for this we revere you.

My soul is waiting for the Lord,
I count on his word.
My soul is longing for the Lord
more than watchman for daybreak.
Let the watchman count on daybreak
and Israel on the Lord.

Because with the Lord there is mercy
and fulness of redemption,
Israel indeed he will redeem
from all its iniquity.

This does not give any indication of how God answers. Attention is focused on the petitioner, who is in considerable distress – in 'the depths' – and is fully aware of his guilt. Like all of us, he is a sinner, but he has the courage and trust to plead with the all-holy God. In doing that, he reveals that he has some knowledge of God's ways and even a certain familiarity with him. He does not attempt to excuse his guilt. Instead, he openly admits it, but boldly reasons with God that, should he mark our guilt, no one would survive. How could God refuse such pleading? He did not wish humanity to perish. On the contrary, he sent his own Son to us as a human baby, and God as Man later died and rose from the dead for us. God is a generous, forgiving Father, as Christ portrayed him so clearly in the parable of the prodigal son. Consequently, the psalmist, relying on God's unchanging nature, can wait for the Lord and count on him. He longs for him, and can end on a joyful note.

In that narrative account of the psalm, there are some ideas suggestive of Christmas and Jesus' birth. The Church goes further and, for Evening Prayer on Christmas Day, displays the psalm to us between special 'antiphons'. Antiphons are verses, usually taken from Scripture, intended to draw our attention to some aspect of the psalm and so to enliven our prayer. The Christmas antiphon is:

With the Lord there is unfailing love.
Great is his power to set men free.

The underlying longing of the psalmist is for God. To see God, he needs freedom from his sins and an ability to love him. The antiphon speaks from God's side, and of his love shown in his becoming a human baby.

32

Conversion

Converts are rather special people. They received a call
from God to change their religion, with all the sufferings
that that may have involved, including for some the loss of
job, position and even family and friends. Most conver-
sions take place over a lengthy period, as indicated in the
beginning of Psalm 39 (which Mendelssohn set to unfor-
gettable music):

> I waited, I waited for the Lord
> and he stooped down to me;
> he heard my cry.

That might be regarded as a continuation of the final
theme of Psalm 146 (see Ch. 14), which declared that 'the
Lord delights... in those who wait for his love.' The time of
waiting and preparation had been fixed by God who knew
what he wanted and hoped for from the other. The person on
trial had no doubt lived through a dry, hard period, but had
inwardly been growing in detachment from self and in trust
in and love for God. There had been a great co-operation
with grace. Then, all was changed, for God took action:

> He drew me from the deadly pit,
> from the miry clay.
> He set my feet upon a rock
> and made my footsteps firm.
>
> He put a new song into my mouth,
> praise of our God.
> Many shall see and fear
> and shall trust in the Lord.

The deadly pit and miry clay may be rather strong images; but, for Catholics, the idea of being set upon a rock is very meaningful. This convert was ready to praise God after all the interior darkness and fear of the past, and his happiness was bound to affect those about him.

In expansion of his own experience, the psalmist continues with an Old Testament type of beatitude:

Happy the man who has placed
his trust in the Lord.

It would have been so easy to have 'gone over to the rebels' during the trial. God is now directly addressed, perhaps by a group of listeners:

How many, O Lord my God,
are the wonders and designs
that you have worked for us;
you have no equal.

The following verses are quoted in the Letter to the Hebrews in a rather difficult passage about the ineffectiveness of the old sacrifices (10:1-10). Jesus' voluntary sacrifice was made once and for all. Then there are declarations of how the psalmist has lived and proclaimed God's justice, help, love and truth. In return, he says:

O Lord, you will not withhold
your compassion from me.
Your merciful love and your truth
will always guard me.

His mood changes, and he makes various complaints. He is beset with innumerable evils; his sins have fallen upon him, and his sight is failing him; but:

O Lord, come to my rescue,
Lord, come to my aid.

That verse resembles the introduction to each of the Hours in the Divine Office, which is:

O God, come to our aid.
O Lord, make haste to help us.

In a spirit of generosity, the psalmist expresses the hope that seekers after God will be glad, but he himself remains in a distressed state:

O let there be rejoicing and gladness
for all who seek you.
Let them ever say: 'The Lord is great',
who love your saving help.

As for me, wretched and poor,
the Lord thinks of me.
You are my rescuer, my help,
O God, do not delay.

We might add to those words a final wish from the Book of Revelation: 'Come, Lord Jesus' (22:20).

33

Desolation

Do you suffer from exposure to an excess of communication? It can be easy to become defensive but then slip into the error of regarding what is read in newspapers as the absolute truth, even when recalled inaccurately.

For example, think of the elderly couple who were in Westminster Cathedral after Vespers on a summer Sunday. The sacristan was clearing the altar in preparation for the 5.30 Mass. Most of the congregation had left, but they remained, sitting near the front. I happened to approach, and the wife asked me when would the ordination start: a certain well known Catholic paper had announced such a service for 4 o'clock that day. It was then after 4.15. She added that the celebrant would be Cardinal Newman. It was nearly the centenary of his death, but I managed, I hope, not to show surprise. I explained that nowadays ordinations to the priesthood usually take place in the parishes. Offering to look up the sacristy's diary, I escaped.

Possibly over-exposure to the media had helped to produce a somewhat deadening effect on that couple's minds. Continual exposure over a long period to some trial in life can also, I have found, produce a similar adverse effect. At one time I had become so accustomed to having to withstand great pressure and behave in certain defensive ways, that I did not notice the accompanying loss in vitality.

That was during the period when I was becoming acquainted with the psalms by reading them slowly in the book of 'Morning and Evening Prayer'. Eventually, in the fourth week of the cycle, for Thursday morning, I read Psalm 142.

Lord, listen to my prayer:
turn your ear to my appeal.
You are faithful, you are just; give answer.
Do not call your servant to judgment
for no one is just in your sight.

The enemy pursues my soul;
he has crushed my life to the ground;
he has made me dwell in darkness
like the dead, long forgotten.
Therefore my spirit fails;
my heart is numb within me.

I remember the days that are past;
I ponder all your works.
I muse on what your hand has wrought
and to you I stretch out my hands.
Like a parched land my soul thirsts for you.

Lord, make haste and answer;
for my spirit fails within me.
Do not hide your face
lest I become like those in the grave.

In the morning let me know your love
for I put my trust in you.
Make me know the way I should walk:
to you I lift up my soul.

Rescue me, Lord, from my enemies;
I have fled to you for refuge.
Teach me to do your will
for you, O Lord, are my God.
Let your good spirit guide me
in ways that are level and smooth.

For your name's sake, Lord, save my life;
in your justice save my soul from distress.

Those words gave me a thrill. I reacted to them personally. I could identify with them. Only then did I casually, out of curiosity, look back to the start of the psalm, and read its title: 'Prayer in desolation'. I was surprised and chilled. My quick, spontaneous reaction was: 'But I am not in desolation. This is my usual state of mind.' Then, giving me some pain, the revelation hit me: 'I really am in desolation, and I did not know it. I have been in desolation for so long.' It was, I would now say, merciful and a sign of God's loving care that I was not able to put a name to my condition until I was ready to be changed.

I wonder how you feel about this. A nun to whom I mentioned this experience declared that it was to be expected that we may not know when we are in desolation. It becomes a habitual state of mind. When I am tired or upset about something, I still tend to withdraw into myself, but that is not like the devastation of desolation. My withdrawal usually ends after a short while, and I am cheerful again.

The psalm contains some hints on how best to react when really desolate. It is obvious that the psalmist had already developed a relationship with God, or rather that God had led him on to do so. He could call on God with touching words, and truthfully indicate, and so face, his problem. He was led to acknowledge his dependence on and need for his Maker, whose works are all wonderful. To him, then, he stretched out both his hands, in a gesture of complete reliance and profound trust. That action in turn showed to him the urgency of his case: he might even despair if he did not soon receive some sign of God's pity and love. He expressed an act of yet further trust: he did not ask for an immediate sign from God, but one in God's own time, 'in the morning'. He humbly accepted that there was some fault on his side, and asked to be shown the way where he was to walk. He would make a new beginning, with God teaching him and his Spirit guiding him. He had experienced a form of conversion.

So-called 'cradle Catholics' need to have a conversion, too, and one way may be through desolation. As his followers, Christ invites us to share something of his agony and death. Later he calls us to experience a resurrection.

34

Confidence (1)

Pontius Pilate 'took some water, washed his hands in front of the crowd and said, "I am innocent of this man's blood. It is your concern."' (Mt 27:24). The Roman governor carried out an easily understandable gesture; but he was trying to disclaim involvement in Jesus' death.

In the offertory of the Mass, the priest washes his hands. Originally, the action may have been a necessary one. Symbolism later became attached to it, and in the Tridentine Rite he used to say verses 6 to 12 of Psalm 25, beginning with the word *Lavabo*:

> To prove my innocence I wash my hands
> and take my place around your altar,
> singing a song of thanksgiving,
> proclaiming all your wonders.

At first sight, this psalm might seem to have been composed by an objectionably self-righteous person:

> Give judgment for me, O Lord:
> for I walk the path of perfection.
> I trust in the Lord; I have not wavered.

The real position, however, may have been that he was asking God to judge him and his cause favourably in a dispute with someone unworthy. Like any good advocate, he pleads his case as strongly and as favourably as he can. He has no hesitation about mentioning his good qualities, and he can do that because he has turned to God and aligned himself with him. He feels that he has no reason to fear the Lord:

Examine me, Lord, and try me;
O test my heart and my mind,
for your love is before my eyes
and I walk according to your truth.

I never take my place with liars
and with hypocrites I shall not go.
I hate the evil-doer's company:
I will not take my place with the wicked.

The psalmist's words become more confident. He
washes, and takes his proper place, which is at God's altar.
He enthuses about God's house where his glory abides.

The following verses present the other side of the argument. There is a request not be swept away with sinners,
and later a petition for redemption, which anticipates that
he will be heard:

As for me, I walk the path of perfection.
Redeem me and show me your mercy.
My foot stands on level ground:
I will bless the Lord in the assembly.

35

Confidence (2)

The motto of Oxford University is *Dominus illuminatio
mea* ('The Lord is my light'). Oxford, however, is sometimes called the home of lost causes. So, it is interesting to
learn that the motto is the beginning of Psalm 26 which
itself shows quite a swing in moods.

The psalmist starts with a bold act of trust in God. Since
the Lord is his light, help and stronghold, would he ever
fear? When the wicked approach to destroy him, they are
the ones who fall. Feeling more confident still, he asserts
that he would not be fearful were a war to break out against
him. He voices his longing: to live continually in God's
Temple and to savour his sweetness. It is God who protects
him and sets him up in safety. He promises to offer 'a
sacrifice of joy'.

Next moment, the mood changes. He is being tested. All
is not pleasant:

O Lord, hear my voice when I call;
have mercy and answer.
Of you my heart has spoken:
'Seek his face.'

It is your face, O Lord, that I seek;
hide not your face...
Though father and mother forsake me,
the Lord will receive me.

It appears that false witnesses have arisen against him.
Almost instinctively, he turns to God with much clamour.
He has not yet reached the point where, knowing from
experience that he can rely fully on God, he can quietly

trust in him. He seems to realise that defect, for he asks:

Instruct me, Lord, in your way;
on an even path lead me.

Christians are taught to expect that their way, following
Christ carrying his cross, will not be easy. While the individual may not see it clearly at the time, the Christian's
path, though, does have a certain evenness to it. Christ is
our light, and through Baptism and Confirmation we have
the Holy Spirit living in each of us, to enlighten and
strengthen us inwardly.

O guide our minds with thy blest light,
with love our hearts inflame;
and with thy strength, which ne'er decays,
confirm our mortal frame.

In turn, we are called by Christ to the amazing work of
ourselves being lights of the world: 'Your light must shine
in the sight of men, so that, seeing your good works, they
may give the praise to your Father in heaven' (Mt 5:16).
Being helped by the Sacraments of the Holy Eucharist and
Reconciliation, we may assist others, and we have the
Church supporting us as our rock and stronghold.

Those truths may seem to be easily spoken but very
distant from our ordinary day-to-day existence. Here the
psalm may help us, for it ends by setting all in an eternal
perspective, and we do not know when we shall be called
to meet God. Until we have trusted fully in him, we shall
not know from our own experience what he can and will do
for us:

I am sure I shall see the Lord's goodness
in the land of the living.
Hope in him, hold firm and take heart.
Hope in the Lord!

36

Confidence (3)

'Unemployment is a scourge.' 'Unemployment is a vocation.' Those apparently opposing views, one negative, the other positive, were expressed by contemporary Catholic bishops. Can they be reconciled?

One thing that I have learned from many fairly short periods of unemployment is a different way of reacting to time. People can be like larks – early to bed, early to rise and lively in the mornings – or like owls – the reverse. There is also an amazing intermediate category, consisting of those who go late to bed and rise early, but who are able to hold down and enjoy very demanding jobs.

Much of our life is geared to the larks, and early rising is often held out as a form of virtue. Hence it came as a shock to me to discover, in shapeless, workless days, that I resembled an owl. Further, I found that depression, very hard to throw off, might accompany unemployment. That could produce a wish, and even the need, to sleep longer. 'What's the point of getting up yet? I know that there's no work for me to do. I'm not needed.'

Being no longer in the rat race, I could, however, begin to slow down and note how many people around me seemed almost continually tired, in a hurry and often rather irritable. On my side, I realised that I might be able to start trying to acquire peace and patience. In words from Psalm 45: 'Be still and know that I am God.'

Unemployment can also produce a more flexible approach to life in each day. Why unnecessarily behave as though part of an institution, such as a boarding school governed by the ringing of bells? So far as is compatible with charity for one's neighbour, it can be relaxing to live according to one's own biological clock. I discovered that the variable rhythms of the seasons can be more congenial than the inflexible beat of a mechanical timepiece.

The lesson I eventually learned was that sometimes we may not be required to toil for our bread, at least, not in the way that we might have expected: Christ has assured us that we are not to worry about our life and what we are to eat, for life means more than food and our heavenly Father knows all our needs (Mt 6:25,32). I hope that those of you who have had personal experience of unemployment will share my affection for the second verse of Psalm 126. It is encouraging, and of course correct, to believe that the unemployed are among those beloved by God.

The first two verses deal with the pointlessness of action without the Lord. Our lives need to be attuned to his wishes for us. An able-bodied person, for example, who does not try as hard as possible to find work but prefers to be unemployed, may be at fault, in contrast to most of those who unwillingly become unemployed. The remainder of the psalm considers the value of children (especially, in the psalmist's eyes, sons) who, in a figurative sense, help to build a house and a city.

If the Lord does not build the house,
in vain do its builders labour;
if the Lord does not watch over the city,
in vain does the watchman keep vigil.

In vain is your earlier rising,
your going later to rest,
you who toil for the bread you eat:
when he pours gifts on his beloved while they slumber.

Truly sons are a gift from the Lord,
a blessing, the fruit of the womb.
Indeed the sons of youth
are like arrows in the hand of a warrior.

O the happiness of the man
who has filled his quiver with these arrows!
He will have no cause for shame
when he disputes with his foes in the gateways.

37

Confidence (4)

Frankly, I must admit that Psalm 130 makes me feel rather uncomfortable. Whatever the nature of the first sin against God may have been, surely pride was in it, with man and woman following their own wishes in preference to the command of God. Since that time, cannot pride be said to have figured in virtually every human fault or failing? It represents a denial to the Supreme Being of what is his due. It can infiltrate, without our realising it, into our seemingly innocent thoughts, words and actions. When unacknowledged, it is still more dangerous.

O Lord, my heart is not proud
nor haughty my eyes.
I have not gone after things too great
nor marvels beyond me.

Truly I have set my soul
in silence and peace.
As a child has rest in its mother's arms,
even so my soul.

O Israel, hope in the Lord
both now and for ever.

How can the psalmist, addressing the Lord confidently, declare that he is not proud? Did he set his sights in life too low, or was only a little genuinely expected of him? He seems to be chiefly concerned with telling the all-knowing God what he is like. That approach contrasts with Mary's. She, the immaculate, began her *Magnificat* (see Ch. 1) with unstinted praise of God, whom she acknowledged as being her Saviour. Only then did she say that he 'looks on his servant in her lowliness' and 'works marvels' for her. Does the psalmist resemble the Pharisee in Jesus' parable (Lk 18:9-14)? He stood self-assertively in the Temple to pray, and detailed to God how exactly he had kept the Law. Jesus concluded that he went home still not at rights with God.

Lay people especially have to make their way in the world. Until we attempt to meet some challenge, we do not know what we can achieve. Our background and expectations may mislead us as to our capacities and capabilities. Again, we may secure a position only to find that circumstances change, and that we can no longer fill it satisfactorily. Life is an on-going pilgrimage, calling for us to venture ourselves, but in union with God and his holy will for us.

Probably that gives the key to this psalm. The writer has learned that in God's will alone is our peace. With that knowledge has come a desire for inner silence, in which he can hear what God says to him. Even if in the past he was agitated, thrusting or proud, having incorrect aims in life, now he can experience inwardly a sense of rest, like an exhausted child sleeping in its mother's arms. He is not childish but childlike, and the image brings to mind beautiful modern pictures of Mary with her infant Son, so drawn that the two seem to blend together.

38

Persecution

'I must get away from it all!' Those words can be said with rather different meanings. The speaker's need may be satisfied with a walk on a common, with a day of recollection or with a holiday in this country or abroad. In each of those cases, the solution is to have a break, and so to return to previous duties, refreshed and reinvigorated. Another interpretation would be given to the words where the speaker wants to leave home or employment or to emigrate. Sometimes that can conceal a lack of the courage necessary to face seemingly overwhelming problems.

The writer of Psalm 54 certainly wanted to get out of a problem, but he used beautiful language to make the point:

> O that I had wings like a dove
> to fly away and be at rest.
> So I would escape far away
> and take refuge in the desert.

The setting by Mendelssohn of those verses ('O for the wings of a dove') is sublime. However, the psalmist did admit to being an escapist at heart.

The start of this psalm recalls that of Psalm 142 (prayer in desolation, see Ch. 33).

> O God, listen to my prayer,
> do not hide from my pleading,
> attend to me and reply;
> with my cares, I cannot rest.

The psalmist is afraid on account of wicked people who bring evil on him. Even death's terror is on him. If he could escape to the desert, he would hasten to find a shelter

from the destructive storm, O Lord,
and from their plotting tongues.

It seems that he is the innocent subject of much slander,
but in turn he may be over-reacting. He claims to see
'nothing but violence and strife in the city... Its streets are
never free from... deceit.' Those are probably exaggerations.

Next, though, he comes to his underlying trouble. It is
so awful that it distorts his vision of life. Pathetically, he
declares that if his harm had been done by an enemy or a
rival, he could have handled the situation:

But it is you, my own companion,
my intimate friend!
How close was the friendship between us.
We walked together in harmony
in the house of God.

The depth of his feeling is shown by his direct address
to that false friend, who will no longer listen to or sympathise with him. However, he knows what to do. He turns
with confidence and prayer to God, and he knows that the
Lord will save him:

He will deliver my soul in peace
in the attack against me:
for those who fight me are many,
but he hears my voice.

Those are moving, helpful verses. Despite outward con-
fusion and uncertainty, with betrayal by someone who
seemed like another self, the psalmist remains aware that
he is still in touch with God, who will continue to guard
and keep him in peace. Without that peace, a dangerous
struggle might ensue between the traitor and himself.
Nevertheless, his position is very hard indeed to bear. As
Christians, we can compare it with Jesus' after his betrayal
by his false apostle, Judas.

Following the questionable example set by some psalms written in times of serious trials, this one calls for revenge on the enemies. God will judge them. There follow sad, harsh words about the traitor who turned against his friends and broke his word:

His speech is softer than butter,
but war is in his heart.
His words are smoother than oil,
but they are naked swords.

That throws into relief the psalmist's advice to those listening to him:

Entrust your cares to the Lord
and he will support you.
He will never allow
the just man to stumble.

It is consoling to think of God supporting us, so that we do not even stumble, let alone fall. However, this assumes that on our side we are genuinely trying to live as God wishes.

The psalmist cannot resist a final rant against his enemies, telling God that he (God) will bring them to death long before their due time. It is necessary for us to keep in mind Jesus' sermon on the mount, when he said: 'Love your enemies and pray for those who persecute you; in this way you will be sons of your Father in heaven, for he causes his sun to rise on bad men as well as good' (Mt 5:44-45).

Finally in the psalm there is a deceptively simple prayer which we may wish to adopt for our own if we are faced with circumstances as distressing as those of the psalmist, or in any event:

O Lord, I will trust in you.

39

Strengthening

Some years ago, I was working happily for a charity. Then rumours began to fly of a possible Government cut in grant-aid. When that eventually happened, my job was made part-time, and I could not afford to continue in it. Fortunately, I found new work before I was too adversely affected.

During this time, I had been praying hard and, and while the unpleasant experience was still fresh in my mind, I read the Missalette before a Sunday Mass. The responsorial psalm contained the words:

On the day I called, you answered;
you increased the strength of my soul.

Previously, the psalms had made little impression on me, partly due to the somewhat difficult translations of the past. However, those words came over to me very strongly and emphatically, as though they were addressed to me and I must take notice of them. Even now when I read them, I respond to them.

In any problem, we are ideally to turn at once, with complete love and trust, to God, and make and renew our intention to put and keep ourselves and our future in his hands. We shall almost certainly need to make more than one such call for help, but we do not have to behave like impatient, spoilt children. We are imperfect, and it is only rarely that we can manage to turn fully away from self, self-pity and even the tendency to despair.

God knows us completely, and still loves us as we are. He answers our first prayer as soon as we make it. So, we help ourselves, and future developments, when we go to him quickly. We may not hear his answer, but he gives it. He may not act in the way or at the time that we wish or expect. His ways are far greater than we can imagine, and he treats each one of us individually, and as a very special person.

The psalmist declared that God increased the strength of his soul. Contrary to some notions, that can be more important than physical strength. God does not necessarily remove the difficulty. He can enable us to see a way out of it or, if there is no such way, to bear it peacefully. He is not niggardly in his help. When we co-operate as fully as we can with him, he will never let us down.

Do those words from the psalm provoke a reaction from you? We all have grave problems from time to time, and it is useful to have had beforehand some training in how to tackle them. We have to acknowledge that we cannot necessarily handle them adequately alone. We need to have a deep realisation that God, who is love, wants to help us, is with us, and is concerned for us, although he may seem distant and we may not feel any immediate response to our appeals to him. He can, and usually does, help us through other people or through a change in circumstances. His immediate way, though, is to give spiritual help, and he comes closer to us than he was before, if we let him do so.

He behaves as a genuine lover. If we co-operate with him, then a loving relationship can begin. In time, we can learn to call on him frequently, and not merely when we need help. We will begin to praise and thank him more spontaneously.

In Holy Week 1989 I realised that the words of Psalm 137 (see also Ch. 44) which had particularly helped me may have helped Jesus as well. In his homily for Morning Prayer (Lauds) on Good Friday in Westminster Cathedral, Cardinal Hume pointed out that the psalms were inspired by the Holy Spirit and were used by Jesus himself. The passion which had been read on Palm Sunday was that of Luke. He told how, in the garden, Jesus had prayed to his Father: 'Father, if you are willing, take this cup away from me. Nevertheless, let your will be done, not mine.' Then his Father answered, and he saw an angel 'coming from heaven to give him strength', not to take away his suffering, for his agony became even greater (Lk 22:42-44). He went on to endure his passion and death, but he rose from the dead, triumphant. He had experienced the truth of the psalmist's words, and he also left us an example of how we should follow in his steps, by praying to God in our time of distress: 'Father, let your will be done, not mine.'

40

Confession

Whatever the crowds and his disciples may have thought at the time, surely Jesus spoke enthusiastically when, sitting on the hill, he taught them the beatitudes. Hard though that teaching may have seemed to be, he would already have lived and experienced its truth. He would have longed for others to share that knowledge with him. The novelty of his teaching, however, was contained in a formula which would have been familiar to his listeners. For instance, Psalm 31 begins:

> Happy the man whose offence is forgiven,
> whose sin is remitted.
> O happy the man to whom the Lord
> imputes no guilt,
> in whose spirit is no guile.

This psalmist is obviously joyful now that his sinful state has ended. He does not say how he had offended God, but his reference to guile may be an indication. According to the Book of Genesis (RSV) Eve told God after the fall: 'The serpent beguiled me' (3:13). Like the devil, deceit is insidious; like a snake's movement, it can glide along silently, and it can grow strong from small, almost disregarded origins. It might also be compared to the deep and wide-ranging root systems of some garden weeds. Unless each root can be found and grubbed up, the weed will survive somewhere to spoil the whole garden's appearance.

We are aware of psychosomatic illnesses, those brought about or aggravated by the reaction of mind on body, say by worrying. The psalmist, living in what we would regard as primitive times, knew about such illnesses too:

I kept it secret and my frame was wasted.

However, he considered that God's hand had been laid heavily upon him. Consistently with this view, he was led to admission of his guilt and repentance, and he longs to share the experience with others:

But now I have acknowledged my sins;
my guilt I did not hide.
I said: 'I will confess
my offence to the Lord.'
And you, Lord, have forgiven
the guilt of my sin.

So let every good man pray to you
in the time of need.

He is so certain that God has forgiven him, that he tells God that that is the case. (This might be contrasted with Psalm 50, see Ch. 30, where the penitent at the end is left still waiting for his confidently expected forgiveness.) He has recovered his integrity and can view life from a true perspective. He asserts that the Lord protects and delivers good people in times of disaster. Even high-reaching flood waters will not reach them.

The tone of the psalm changes. The psalmist had given evidence of his rescue directly to God. Now he addresses himself to all good people, advising that they should approach the Lord with trust. He claims that:

Many sorrows has the wicked

while indicating that the just have a protection of loving mercy. The psalm finishes as it had begun, with an outburst of joy due to the action of God:

Rejoice, rejoice in the Lord,
exult, you just!
O come, ring out your joy,
all you upright of heart.

How lovely that this is one of the penitential psalms!

41

Holy Eucharist

God the Son almost certainly made use of psalms when teaching the apostles and trying to open their minds. Near the end of Luke's gospel, we read: 'I said, while I was still with you (that is, during his public ministry), that everything written about me in the Law of Moses, in the Prophets and in the Psalms, has to be fulfilled' (24:44). Which psalms might he have referred to, when foretelling his sufferings, death and resurrection, and the subsequent world-wide diffusion of the Good News?

Psalm 21 (see Ch. 23) would be a strong probability. Hanging on the cross, Jesus managed to gasp out the beginning of it: 'My God, my God, why have you forsaken me?' Many of the following verses are prophetic or figurative, and give recognisable pictures of aspects of the passion.

Psalm 117 (see Ch. 27) would be a possibility. One part of it is interpreted as alluding to the resurrection:

> The stone which the builders rejected
> has become the corner stone.
> This is the work of the Lord,
> a marvel in our eyes.
> This day was made by the Lord;
> we rejoice and are glad.

Jesus quoted from that in the course of a discussion with the chief priests and scribes about the nature of his authority. After Pentecost, Peter directly applied to him the words about the corner stone.

A psalm used at Evening Prayer on Good Friday and Holy Saturday and also for several occasions during the year, is Psalm 115. We can see that some parts of it were prophetic. Like Psalm 117, it is one of a group of psalms of praise recited by Jews at great feasts. In view of what Matthew and Mark tell us in their gospels, we can safely say that Jesus and the apostles sang it at the end of the Passover supper on Maundy Thursday, before leaving the upper room to go to the Mount of Olives.

> I trusted, even when I said:
> 'I am sorely afflicted,'
> and when I said in my alarm:
> 'No man can be trusted.'
>
> How can I repay the Lord
> for his goodness to me?
> The cup of salvation I will raise;
> I will call on the Lord's name.
>
> My vows to the Lord I will fulfil
> before all his people.
> O precious in the eyes of the Lord
> is the death of his faithful.
>
> Your servant, Lord, your servan, am I;
> you have loosened my bonds.
> A thanksgiving sacrifice I make:
> I will call on the Lord's name.
>
> My vows to the Lord I will fulfil
> before all his people,
> in the courts of the house of the Lord,
> in your midst, O Jerusalem.

Isaiah had prophesied about the Suffering Servant of the Lord. Christ was 'sorely afflicted', and was betrayed for money by one of the apostles and out of fear by their leader. Although on the cross he expressed a sense of abandonment by God, his trust in his Father surely did not fail. At the end of his life, he committed his Spirit into the

Father's hands. The words come from Psalm 30 (see Ch. 24), which continues: 'It is you who will redeem me, Lord.' On Easter morning God loosened the bonds of his Servant, who rose from the dead.

So, as Psalm 115 says, Jesus would make a thanksgiving sacrifice before all the people. He had already instituted the Eucharist on Maundy Thursday, and the Mass is a continual re-presentation of Calvary. In the Tridentine Rite, just before receiving the Precious Blood from the chalice, the celebrant prayed in Latin: 'What return shall I make to the Lord for all that he has given me? I will take the chalice of salvation and invoke the name of the Lord.'

As Christians, we are called and empowered (if we co-operate) to resemble Jesus. May Psalm 115 help us? Initially, the psalmist acknowledges that he had some serious affliction without saying whether it was physical, emotional, mental or spiritual. Thus the psalm can easily be applied to many situations. He was afraid, and that made him blurt out in a too sweeping, and hence false, generalisation, that no one could be trusted. However, with the help of grace he held onto his trust in God, who 'is faithful for ever' (Psalm 116, see Ch. 47). Psalm 115 is one of thanksgiving, a looking back at the past trouble when making an offering in fulfilment of a promise. God likes to be thanked. We know that from Jesus' reaction at the time that nine cured lepers neglected to do so. During our lives, he frees us from many forms of bondage, and he always yearns for us to turn to him with immediate gratitude and praise. The Mass is the best way for us to respond to his longing.

42

Thanksgiving (1)

When I had no more to say, he asked would I like to join him in prayer. I agreed, and waited for about half a minute as he stood with head bowed. Then he began to pray quietly.

He spoke spontaneously and fluently to Our Father, bringing in by name those who had caused my problem. Strikingly, he also thanked God with simple and sincere words for the problem and for all those involved. At first I could not understand. Very gradually I felt soothed and peace returned to me. He was a lay Evangelical Christian who died suddenly a few years later. He was well prepared.

Has it ever occurred to you to thank God for a great difficulty when in the midst of it and without sight of any solution? Jesus in effect did that before he raised Lazarus to life. 'Father, I thank you for hearing my prayer' (Jn 11:41). The idea of thanks for harsh circumstances sounds remarkable to us at first. All around us the easy, comfortable life is preached.

However, for our own sakes God can allow us to be tried.

> For you, O God, have tested us,
> you have tried us as silver is tried: ...
> we went through fire and through water
> but then you brought us relief.

That extract is from Psalm 65, which is one of thanksgiving and which had already urged everyone to say to God: 'How tremendous your deeds!'

Psalm 138 (see Ch. 3) goes further and joyfully invites God to test us.

O search me, God, and know my heart.
O test me and know my thoughts.
See that I follow not the wrong path
and lead me in the path of life eternal.

God knows all things, and such an invitation might
seem superfluous and foolhardy, were it not for the psalmist's experience of God's past dealings, his utter confidence in him, and his happy acceptance that his loving
Father knows him through and through. He makes himself
open to God's action in a great act of trust. For the psalmist
a trial by God was never more than he could bear and the
result was greater closeness to him. If, through weakness or
error, he went astray, God would not let him down but
would continue to lead him to eternal life. On the other
hand, this cannot be taken as authority for us to anticipate
God's will and bring trials on ourselves unnecessarily.
That could be courting tragedy.

Normally we can thank God for less dramatic happenings in our lives. In the daily Morning Prayer we anticipate
having both happiness and sufferings. Realising that we
and all things come from God, or that he permits all that
happens, we can experience a gradual growth in an outlook
of thanksgiving leading to joy.

Cry out with joy to the Lord, all the earth.
Serve the Lord with gladness.
Come before him, singing for joy.

Know that he, the Lord, is God.
He made us, we belong to him,
we are his people, the sheep of his flock.

Go within his gates, giving thanks.
Enter his courts with songs of praise.
Give thanks to him and bless his name.

Indeed, how good is the Lord,
eternal his merciful love.
He is faithful from age to age.

There are no reservations in Psalm 99. The psalmist
encourages all to join with him, and we can feel his joy
centuries later. We have greater reasons for joy too, because we know that we have been redeemed from death by
Jesus. We can regard our trials as invitations by him to us
to join in his passion, death and resurrection. They can
become a series of deaths to self so that each time we may
rise to live more fully for and with God.

That psalm was composed for a procession to the Temple. When we go to church, it is often for the celebration of
Mass, which is also called the Eucharist, meaning Thanksgiving. In the Eucharist we give God thanks for everything,
and with Jesus we can become a thank-offering to the
Father. Like Jesus at the Last Supper, the celebrant at Mass
takes the bread, and then the cup, giving thanks before he
consecrates each. We are caught up into that action for our
own benefit and for that of the whole world.

43

Thanksgiving (2)

'And she said to me: ... And I said to her: ...' Surely you have occasionally overheard this vivid kind of talk, where a person relates in some detail to a long-suffering friend exactly what happened on a certain occasion. The speaker may be wound up – full of the need to impart this news – and carry on rapidly and almost breathlessly for a while, fearing an interruption from the patient listener before all has been disclosed. An outsider might find some amusement in this situation, but could hardly doubt the sincerity of the raconteur.

How might we ourselves react were we to overhear someone declaring: 'And I called on God, O save me!' Perhaps we might instinctively look hard and wonder: 'Is this a fanatic?' How was this person dressed and behaving? What words would follow? Unfortunately, nowadays it can be easy not to bring God into our troubles, but to try to manage in our own way.

Hundreds of years ago, a psalmist enthused (in Psalm 114) about how God had saved him in response to his call, even his scream, for deliverance. The account has the hallmarks of authenticity. A comparison might be made with the curing by Jesus of a blind man near Jericho as narrated by Luke (18:35-43).

The psalmist begins by emphasising that now he loves God better than before. He seems more aware that God is a Person, not a mere powerful entity. A new, deeper relationship has begun. We could say that the Holy Spirit had intervened.

We are not told exactly what the trial was, but it was probably due to a natural cause such as a very severe, and maybe painful, illness. The psalmist claims that he was caught by distress, with death waiting to pounce. What was he to do? He had come to the end of his resources. He realised that he was helpless. He admits that he had simplicity; but his was the simplicity which goes with profundity and not the simplicity of a fool. He was uncomplicated and trusting. So, from his inmost being, he could humbly call on God, as his Lord, rely totally on him, and know that, despite appearances, all would be well.

Again, the psalmist does not indicate how God responded. Whatever actually happened to avert the evil, he knew that the Supreme Person had intervened. There had not been a magical response to a set formula of petition. It had been, in a way, so easy. There was no need now to detail too much. The approach could be different. The speaker wants to communicate to his listeners some sense of the spiritual benefit of his experience. He hopes that they will join with him in praising God. He is full of God, not of self. He wants to direct the attention of others away from self and to God. Inwardly, he can relax and be at peace, realising that he has become closer to his Lord than he was before.

I love the Lord for he has heard
the cry of my appeal;
for he turned his ear to me
in the day when I called him.

They surrounded me, the snares of death,
with the anguish of the tomb;
they caught me, sorrow and distress.
I called on the Lord's name.

O Lord my God, deliver me!

How gracious is the Lord, and just;
our God has compassion.
The Lord protects the simple hearts;
I was helpless so he saved me.

137

Turn back, my soul, to your rest
for the Lord has been good;
he has kept my soul from death,
my eyes from tears
and my feet from stumbling.

I will walk in the presence of the Lord
in the land of the living.

This psalm (Psalm 114) and Psalm 115 (see Ch. 41) are
combined as Psalm 116 in the Hebrew numbering system.
The Church uses them, one after the other, as the psalms of
Evening Prayer II for several martyrs.

44

Thanksgiving (3)

In the Fens, about 25 miles North of Cambridge, is situated the town of March. The spire of its mediaeval church can be seen quite a distance away over the flat countryside. The dedication is to an obscure Saxon saint, Wendreda, but the interior is memorable. Choirs of angels, nearly 200 in all, carved of wood with widely spreading wings, decorate the magnificent hammerbeam roof. Other old churches in East Anglia contain lesser displays of angels, and the similarity is such that many were probably made by the same team of travelling craftsmen. Fortunately, the carvings were placed too high for the seventeenth century iconoclast of the area, William Dowsing, to have destroyed with his arrows and shot. We can still continue to enjoy the presence of these angels.

Nowadays, the actual existence of angels is not widely accepted. It is, however, a comforting thought that powerful spirits were chosen by God to protect our towns and ourselves. Their main duty, though, is to give praise to him. The Jewish psalmist had no doubts about that when he wholeheartedly and movingly thanked God (in Psalm 137, see also Ch. 39) for his amazing goodness to him, in strengthening him spiritually just when he needed it.

I thank you, Lord, with all my heart,
you have heard the words of my mouth.
In the presence of the angels I will bless you.
I will adore before your holy temple.

I thank you for your faithfulness and love
which excel all we ever knew of you.
On the day I called, you answered;
you increased the strength of my soul.

All earth's kings shall thank you
when they hear the words of your mouth.
They shall sing of the Lord's ways:
'How great is the glory of the Lord!'

The Lord is high yet he looks on the lowly
and the haughty he knows from afar.
Though I walk in the midst of affliction
you give me life and frustrate my foes.

You stretch out your hand and save me,
your hand will do all things for me.
Your love, O Lord, is eternal,
discard not the work of your hands.

The psalmist can hardly contain his enthusiasm. Nothing like this, he declares, has ever before happened to an Israelite, and he wants to enlarge the numbers of those praising God to include all kings on earth. Immediately, that view is qualified, for the great God reverses ordinary human values by being closer to the humble than to the proud. This assertion is made impersonally. By contrast, the Lord is addressed directly and even familiarly but reverently in most of what goes before and in all that follows. The psalmist now makes an act of trust in God, that even should he be surrounded by troubles, he will survive.

The image of God's hand stretched out to help and save brings to mind incidents from Jesus' life, for example, his cure of a leper (Mk 1:40-43) and his rescue of Peter sinking when he had tried to walk on the water too (Mt 14:28-31). The insecurity expressed in the psalm's final line could be compared to Peter's lack of faith. God would never himself discard his work; like a potter, he wants to refashion misshapen human beings. We have further assurance in St Paul's Second Letter to Timothy (2:11-13):

Here is a saying that you can rely on: ...
If we hold firm, then we shall reign with him.
If we disown him, then he will disown us.
We may be unfaithful, but he is always faithful,
for he cannot disown his own self.

45

Praise of works of God

Even in its present state, the Colosseum at Rome, which was built in the first hundred years after Christ, can be described as great, majestic and even glorious. It can also be regarded as fearful, because here many early Christians were martyred by being thrown to wild beasts, while the watching crowds jeered and yelled.

Does it seem at all strange or unfitting that we can use many of the adjectives contained in the preceding paragraph to describe God's works? The Romans, talented in civil engineering, could erect massive but primarily practical buildings. The power of God, who created everything that exists out of nothing, is of an infinitely greater kind and quality; but we lack the words to talk adequately about it. So, if our speech falters, we can the better remember that God and his works are far greater than we can express. Our attempts, though, can give him praise, especially when they are made through Jesus to the Father.

After a promise to thank God, one hymn of praise, Psalm 110, continues

Great are the works of the Lord;
to be pondered by all who love them.

We cannot truly love Roman ruins in the same way that we can love what God has made, for in some manner he is in all that he has made (especially people) and he is love. In daily life, it is hard for us to recognise that immanence of God. Sometimes we may sense it; silent prayer is the best means to reach some small notion of it. Mary can lead us in this. After Jesus' birth and the shepherds' visit to Bethlehem, 'she treasured all these things and pondered them in her heart' (Lk 2:19).

142

Majestic and glorious his work,
his justice stands firm for ever.
He makes us remember his wonders.
The Lord is compassion and love.

The psalmist recalls God's wonders done to save his
people, and briefly lists some of them: the provision of
food (manna and quails in the desert), the faithful remembrance of his covenant (in contrast to the people's behaviour), the gift of the Promised Land. He further praises the
precepts of the Law as being sure, everlasting and true.

As Christians, we have so much more for which to
thank and praise God. When we are aware of his closeness
to us and his care for us, we can see how he feeds and
supports us in every way, physically and spiritually. He
never misleads or forgets us: he could not do so. He wants
us ultimately to join him in his own everlasting life. In the
meantime, we enjoy the help and support of his Church.

Holy his name, to be feared.

To fear the Lord is the first stage of wisdom;
all who do so prove themselves wise.
His praise shall last for ever!

This is not the painful kind of fear which was experienced by the Christian martyrs. It is a proper reverence and
respect for the Supreme Being and Creator upon whom we,
as creatures, are completely dependent, but who, in his
love for us, has given us a certain freedom. Mary, again,
received insights about this. In her *Magnificat* (see Ch. 1)
she declared (Lk 1:50):

His mercy is from age to age,
on those who fear him.

46

Praise – from creation

Before Vatican II, Catholics tended to think of their religion as being primarily a personal matter between each individual and God. Since then, the Church has stressed that there is another aspect of religion as well, that of community. We are involved with each other. We do not live in isolation. What we do and what we are, whether we realise it or not, affects others.

Partly on account of their difficult history, the Jews had a strong bonding between each other. They could also invite others to join with them in joyful praise of the creator. Psalm 148 is a splendid example of that, and the author's enthusiasm can still be felt especially when the psalm is chanted.

It follows a fairly strict order with some artistic touches. Praise of the Lord from the heavens, from his angels and all his hosts is first invited. Next, the wish is expressed that the material heavens, sun, moon, shining stars and the waters above the heavens, will praise the Lord's name.

> He commanded: they were made.
> He fixed them for ever.

Turning to the lower creation, there is a list including sea creatures, all oceans, lightning and hail, snow and mist, 'stormy winds that obey his word', mountains and hills, trees, beasts, reptiles and birds. Humanity, too, is listed in an order, and the Gentiles would be included:

> all earth's kings and peoples,
> earth's princes and rulers;
> young men and maidens,
> old men together with children.

Let them praise the name of the Lord
for he alone is exalted.
The splendour of his name
reaches beyond heaven and earth.

Finally, attention is given to the Israelites. As the people
of God's New Covenant, we could read this verse as relating to ourselves as well:

He exalts the strength of his people.
He is the praise of all his saints,
of the sons of Israel,
of the people to whom he comes close.

47

Praise (1)

'My dad's got ...' 'That's nothing! My dad's got ...' Childish 'one-upmanship', but is not it all too easy to carry the approach into adult life? However, in making comparisons, we would probably be concerned with material things or with human talents or position. It would come strangely to us to make comparisons of gods.

That is what could and did happen very long ago, and always to the advantage of the one true God of Israel. For example, here are some extracts from the second part of Psalm 113 (Psalm 134 contains similar sentiments):

But our God is in the heavens;
he does whatever he wills.
Their (i.e. the heathens') idols are silver and gold,
the work of human hands.

They have mouths but they cannot speak;
they have eyes but they cannot see;
they have ears but they cannot hear;
they have nostrils but they cannot smell.

The psalmist hurls out a warning:

Their makers will come to be like them
and so will all who trust in them.

The tone of the writing then softens to an appeal coupled with an affirmation:

Sons of Israel, trust in the Lord;
he is their help and their shield.

When it was obvious that the visible foreign gods had been man-made, there was little problem. The situation could be different where an invisible Supreme Being was acknowledged but beliefs about him differed. Was he one? Were there three Persons in the one? Could one such Person become man?

While I was an undergraduate, a branch of the World Congress of Faiths was started at the university. Able speakers from many faiths gave talks about their beliefs, which were all sincerely held, but differed widely from one another. I recall talks on Zoroastrianism by a Persian, Taoism by an eminent scholar and Baha'i (previously unknown to me – it had attracted many who disliked Church structures), besides ones on the Church of England and the Roman Catholic Church. The last was given by a monk who had not been properly briefed. He gave a very learned lecture on a mediaeval book, Hilton's *Scale of Perfection*, but responded well to broadly based questions afterwards. I remember at some stage suddenly thinking: 'But these people believe in the same God as I do!' That statement may have needed some qualification, but it was quite a revelation to someone who had been brought up in the semi-ghetto atmosphere of the pre-Vatican II Catholic Church.

That was a twentieth century revelation. How wonderful that the writer of one psalm (Ps 116) hundreds of years before Christ, could invite all the world, including the pagans, to praise the Lord for his love and faithfulness to Israel. That was a primitive, unusual ecumenical gesture. The psalm is the shortest of the Psalter, and is very beautiful. You may well know it in Latin: 'Laudate Dominum omnes gentes'. It is often sung at Benediction. There is also a superb setting by Mozart in his *Solemn Vespers for a Confessor*. We would now interpret the psalm as showing God's love for all.

O praise the Lord, all you nations,
acclaim him all you peoples!

Strong is his love for us;
he is faithful for ever.

48

Praise (2)

How often do lay Catholics praise God on weekdays? If we have offered our work to him, we can praise him through that; but there are the short or long periods of time when, for one reason or another, we have no work. Does praising God come easily in such circumstances?

According to Ignatius Loyola, who founded the Jesuits, we were created to praise, reverence and serve God our Lord, and by that means to save our souls. We can serve God by serving him in other people. If we are to praise him here, even before we reach our destiny of heaven, would it not be sensible (from a human viewpoint) to start practising such joyful praising as soon as possible?

Perhaps use of the psalms could assist us, for they were composed primarily as poems of praise of God. In fact, they were intended to be sung rather than said. They can speak to us as we are. For instance, Psalm 85 begins with a moan:

> Turn your ear, O Lord, and give answer
> for I am poor and needy.

Only later comes the verse:

> I will praise you, Lord my God, with all my heart
> and glorify your name for ever.

It can be such a relief to read a prayer where one is treated as human, with all one's failings and imperfections, but still is encouraged and drawn on to adoration.

Pure adoration is very hard for us to achieve. We can be led to it, with grace, through thanksgiving and love. Psalm

103 (see Ch. 12) which enthuses about the glories of creation and God's care for it, begins and ends with the words:

Bless the Lord, my soul!

On a higher level still I would place Psalm 150, the last in the Psalter:

Praise God in his holy place,
praise him in his mighty heavens.
Praise him for his powerful deeds,
praise his surpassing greatness.

O praise him with sound of trumpet,
praise him with lute and harp.
Praise him with timbrel and dance,
praise him with strings and pipes.

O praise him with resounding cymbals,
praise him with clashing of cymbals.
Let everything that lives and that breathes
give praise to the Lord.

In vivid and picturesque language, that psalm tells us where, why and how to praise God. Although we live in a materialistic society, we benefit from having nearly twenty centuries of Christianity behind us. We know far more than the psalmist did about God's dealings with humanity. We can praise God present in each consecrated Host as well as present in the still unfolding wonders of the universe. We can praise him for the humility of his Son, in becoming Man, suffering, dying and rising again for us and for our salvation. We can praise him for the orchestra of his people, in which each of us plays a different instrument but the music is unbelievably harmonious. We, with our voices, can also sing and praise him in the name of the whole of creation.

To help sustain our enthusiasm, we would do well to

look out for and note the little, everyday signs of God's loving care for us. The nineteenth century Jesuit poet, Gerard Manley Hopkins, could give glory to God for dappled things, list some, and then invite us to praise him. The exclamation, 'Glory to God', can become for us a prayer of the deepest meaning. We can make the *Gloria Patri*, which we normally recite at the end of every psalm, into our very own song of loving response to the wonders we ourselves notice.

Conclusion

If the psalms can help us to develop and enlarge our relationship with God, by assisting us to open out with trust and love to him and to his influence, can they also enable us to come closer to him and even to meet him? That question, however, has been put the wrong way round, for it is always God, the First Being, who initiates. Our part is to try to be prepared and ready to meet and welcome him however and whenever he may appear. We are to be expectant and watchful. In that, too, we need his help, and he gladly gives it to us when we ask him for it. This preparation of ourselves involves letting God take over, as it were, layer after layer of self so that he may become more and more fully the Lord of us. Another name for that process is the living of the Christian life.

In practice, there are at least three ways in which the psalms may help our pilgrimage to God.

In the first place, when reading a psalm, we may find that a sentence, phrase or just a word strikes us, for in general we tend to notice things when we need them or are subconsciously looking for them. The Holy Spirit himself may be directly touching us too. Whatever the reason, it can be rewarding to make a mental note of the outstanding piece, and to allow the mind to ponder on it at intervals during a day or so. If we neglect to do that, we may miss an opportunity; the same words may not even attract us on a later occasion. Many psalms are compressed in style and contain so many ideas that we can find a large source of topics for meditation in them. It is good for us to accumulate a great store of these, for use when our minds are less stimulated.

Secondly, the Church has recognised from its early days that the saying of psalms regularly is desirable. Following the reforms of Vatican II and the use of new English translations for the psalms, many lay people now recite Morning and Evening Prayer whether in a group or alone. Those Prayers form the most important parts of the Divine Office. Their aim is to promote the worship of God throughout the day. When we worship him, we fulfil the main purpose of our existence. The Divine Office is arranged in a four-week cycle, with variations for different seasons in the Church's year and for important feasts. This gives a framework of stability filled with details of much variety, colour and beauty. Besides psalms the Prayers include scriptural readings and intercessions.

Thirdly, the incorporation of a responsorial psalm into the Mass can help us to see further meanings and connections in the First Reading and the Gospel, leading on to the celebration of the Eucharist.

When the two apostles were on the way to Emmaus, they certainly did not expect to meet Jesus again. They were not prepared when he joined them, and did not recognise him. They had not recognised him either in the Scriptures, including the psalms; but he lovingly explained to those dull men the relevant passages about himself. For them, all did not become clear until he gave the eucharistic signs of taking, blessing, breaking and giving the bread, but immediately he vanished (Lk 24:13-32).

God may seem to treat us at times in a similar way. He may let us have an enlightening idea from a psalm and in that he may seem to be particularly close. During other periods we may find that few such lights come. That does not matter. God continues to hold us fast. He gives us what spiritual food we need. He draws us to himself in his way and in his time.

Index of titles

Index of psalms

Note: References in **bold** type are to the sections which deal with the psalms.

Note: The penitential psalms are Pss 6, 31, 37, 50, 101, 129 and 142.

HOW TO READ THE GOSPELS
Historicity and truth in the Gospels and Acts

Peter Schmidt

How *should* a Gospel be read? This book offers a solution to this often discouraging question by providing the necessary basic information and intellectual insight. The author gives his readers three important keys to help open the door to a correct understanding of the relationship of the Gospels' 'historical factuality' and 'their truth'. First, soemthing which 'didn't really happen' can still be 'true'. The second key offers a well-founded yet accessible insight into the growth and mutual relationships of the Gospels. The 'synoptic question' is not merely an optional scholarly pastime, but is extremely important for a correct interpretation of the text. Finally, the third key illuminates the individual characteristics (structure, work method, opinions, goals, etc.) of the four Gospels (and Acts) separately.

The book is also intended as a 'workbook'. In many places reading exercises or practical applications are suggested. They form a learning aid for study groups and their leaders.

PETER SCHMIDT (Ghent, 1945) was ordained priest for the diocese of Ghent in 1971. He studied classical languages in Louvain and biblical theology in Rome. He has been a professor in the diocesan seminary in Ghent since 1973, where he teaches Old and New Testament exegesis and Biblical languages.

ISBN 085439 430 3   205 pp   £10.95

THE TREASURES OF JESUS

Alan Robinson

This book is a thoughtful commentary about the Sermon on the Mount, which is a collection of the sayings of Jesus of Nazareth to be found in Matthew's Gospel (Chapters 5-7). The Sermon is one the world's most important documents because it records the sayings of a person who, at the very least, was a great religious teacher. Christians, of course, believe that Jesus was more than that, in fact, that he was the Son of God.

The author comments on the text, drawing out its meaning, but also discuss the implications of the sayings of Jesus for today. At the end of each section there are three suggested readings from other parts of the Bible. Each set of readings illuminates one of the sayings of Jesus and they are specially chosen to take up the same theme. Also, there is an appropriate prayer after each section.

The book can be used by individuals to learn more about the implications of what Jesus said in his Sermon. They will be able then to meditate on the sayings. At the same time, the material is suitable for study groups and certainly the sayings, together with the author's comments, do stimulate discussion.

ALAN ROBINSON studied theology at New College, University of Edinburgh. He was formerly Principal Lecturer in Theology and Religious Studies at the Derbyshire College of Higher Education (now the University of Derby). He has previously published children's books, theological articles and poetry.

ISBN 085439 466 4   142 pp   £5.95

YAHWEH:
SHEPHERD OF THE PEOPLE
Pastoral symbolism in the Old Testament

Elena Bosetti

What did Israel experience in its "life of strangers and nomads" when God revealed himself to them as a Shepherd? How does Israel re-interpret and live out that experience? What does this pastoral symbolism evoke that it continues thousands of years later, and in situations so different, even in a society advanced in technology?

The image of the shepherd runs across the whole Scripture from Genesis to the Apocalypse. It is one of the most precious images in biblical spirituality.

In *Yahweh: Shepherd of the People* the author traces the socio-cultural milieu within which the *pastoral symbolism* was formed. In the first part she presents three couples (Jacob and Rachel, Moses and Miriam, David and Abigail) who illustrate the wealth of reciprocity within the pastoral dimension. She goes on to explain how these people and the *symbolism of the staff and the tent* have constantly inspired the message of the prophets, the prayer of Israel, and the reflections of the sages.

The image of the shepherd comes to describe the behaviour of God, his "taking care" of his people. God loves them, guides, nurtures and defends them, becomes their companion on the journey. For this reason Israel can sing with confidence the psalm: "The Lord is my shepherd, I shall not want."

085439 441 9   174pp (170x230mm)   £9.50